www.penguin.co.uk

You've Got to Laugh
Stories from a Life Lived to the Full

ALISON HAMMOND

PENGUIN BOOKS

TRANSWORLD PUBLISHERS

Penguin Random House, One Embassy Gardens,
8 Viaduct Gardens, London SW11 7BW
www.penguin.co.uk

Transworld is part of the Penguin Random House group of companies
whose addresses can be found at global.penguinrandomhouse.com

First published in Great Britain in 2021 by Bantam Press
an imprint of Transworld Publishers
Penguin paperback edition published 2022

A CIP catalogue record for this book
is available from the British Library.

ISBN 9780552178563

Printed and bound in Great Britain by Clays Ltd, Elcograf S.p.A.

The authorized representative in the EEA is Penguin Random House Ireland,
Morrison Chambers, 32 Nassau Street, Dublin DO2 YH68.

Penguin Random House is committed to a sustainable
future for our business, our readers and our planet. This book
is made from Forest Stewardship Council® certified paper.

For you, Mum 💕 Maria

Hiya, babes!

How are you? It's so nice that you've bought my book. Thank you, and welcome to the world of Alison Hammond. I'm an author, everyone! Can you believe it? I've actually written a memoir – I feel so honoured to have had this chance. And do you know what? I've discovered that I really enjoy writing. Result!

I expect you're wondering what to expect as you travel with me on this journey through my life. As you'd probably imagine, there are high and low points along the way, because that's the way life is. I'll also be taking you a little bit sideways and diagonally, babes, just to break up the journey, so you'll be reading about my loves and my losses, and a little bit of gossip. Obviously I want to share the klutzy and the showbizzy moments that will give you lots of giggles and lols. The celebs, the men, the breakages . . .

I'm not saying my life has been a comedy fusion of mishaps, but I've had some hilarious moments and I do sometimes wonder how I got from there to here in one piece.

As this was my first ever book, I decided to start right at the beginning. Yes, this book begins with me being born! I've never read a book that dives straight in like that – and it just made sense to me. It's simple and it's good, and the best things in life are simple and good, I find. After I've dealt with my momentous birth, I sketch a path through my Birmingham childhood to give you some insight into my family background. This is where you'll read about how my late mum Maria's love, values and morals made me the person I am today, as well as my lucky break into acting and performing, which set me up for the job I do now. It's all about how I became ME! That's the book. It's that simple.

My life hasn't been plain sailing – but you've got to make the most of the times when the wind doesn't blow, haven't you? Maybe your boat nearly sinks or you literally just get stuck on dry land and can't even launch. You're grounded, beached. I won't lie, I had a few years in my twenties when it seemed like nothing at all was happening – but do you know what? Something *was* happening. I just didn't realize it, because I was too busy trying to earn a living and stay afloat. I had absolutely no idea that everything I was doing was leading me towards a show called *This Morning*, but it was.

As you'll see, there was a 'sliding doors' moment along the way when I very nearly chose to go in another direction altogether. For a while, I deeply regretted the decision I took: it felt as if my boat had capsized and I was never going to set sail again. Not in my wildest dreams was I expecting to end up with a career on daytime telly. It's so weird how life turns out sometimes.

I've been on TV quite a lot in the last twenty years and, to be honest, I've had some good and bad experiences. I've been on some shows that have been the best fun ever, but I've also had some calamities and one or two down-right catastrophes – at least, they felt like catastrophes at the time. Through good times and bad, I kept on going, with the love of my mum and my wonderful family to support me and keep me positive. Wait, I haven't even mentioned my son Aidan yet – he's my world! The day Aidan was born was purely and simply the best day of my life. But I can't lie: when I saw his funny little newborn babyface for the first time, I had to laugh.

I don't think you'll be surprised to learn that sex, drugs and rock and roll are not a part of this book: I'm saving those for the sequel, lol. But I have been through a series of ups and downs with my size and weight, and here's where you'll learn how I feel about taking up space in the world. I also found myself writing about how I've dealt with criticism: I haven't laughed it all off, but I do feel very strongly that there's no point trying to please other people all the time. Just follow your gut and do what you think is right.

After reading my memoir, you'll be able to dissect me and understand what makes me tick. It's quite exposing for me, but I'm hoping that people can learn from my mistakes and understand why I am who I am. Take care of this book because it is a little piece of me – it's like having me in a book! I'm hoping that every time you open it you'll find a reason to laugh. Whether things are good or bad, you've just got to laugh, because ultimately, one day, this is all going to be over. Like it or not, we are going to die, so why not just embrace life, enjoy it and laugh along the way . . . ?

In my job, as in life, I treat everybody the same. Because

over the years I've realized that it doesn't matter how rich or famous people are: ultimately, we're all human beings and we all want to laugh and connect with somebody else; we all want love. So, whoever you are – whether you're Denzel Washington or Denzel *from* Washington, whether you're Sarah from Lancashire, or Belinda from Carlisle – sit back, relax and enjoy!

love,
Alison xx

1. THE MAKING OF ME

I had a happy childhood filled with love, laughter and my mother's delicious cooking, with the occasional hug from Muhammad Ali, my namesake. But, first, something very important had to happen to make it all possible . . .

Beginnings

At 6 p.m. on 5 February 1975, I bounced into this world: my big, Black, naked, seven-pound, one-ounce self.

Well, I thought I'd start this book off with the most amazing day of my life, guys! And obviously it was the day I was born at the Sorrento Maternity Hospital in Mosley, Bimingham, which is now a retirement community – so you never know, if I stay in Birmingham for the rest of my life, I might end my days there as well!

It was just me, my mum and a midwife called Natasha in the delivery room that day. Can you guess what my middle name is? Yes, I'm Alison *Natasha* Hammond, after the midwife who helped my mum give birth to me. I don't know a single thing about this woman, but obviously she was a very, very special person for my mum to give me her name.

That was my mum: she was full of joy and made friends everywhere she went, whatever she was doing, even when she was in the middle of giving birth to me.

When I came along, my sister Saundra was nine and my brother Nicholas was eight. Saundra loved babies and straight away treated me like I was her baby doll, but Nicky was devastated when my mum brought me home from the hospital.

'I don't want her here,' he complained. 'She's going to eat all the food!'

He was right. I did eat all the food (wink). I'm only joking – although I would have done, given half the chance, because my mum's cooking was so, so good.

My mum, my brother and sister were living in a flat in a tower block in Nechells when I was born, but the arrival of a third child meant the council gave Mum a three-bedroom house in Kingstanding, a whole other area of Birmingham. Result!

'I prayed for you,' my mum used to tell me. 'I prayed so hard for you, and when you came out you were beautiful. I was so happy.'

I don't think the house was the reason why she prayed to have me, but it was a nice bonus. She was over the moon to move from the ninth floor of a tower block into a brand-spanking-new home with a garage, a garden at the front and a garden at the back for her children to run about in.

My mum Maria was a social bunny. She loved entertaining and being the centre of attention. Even in her last days, her house was crammed with people coming to see her, and it was the same when we were growing up. She was a lovely, kind woman who brought everybody in the family together.

Ours was a house of entertainment on the weekends when I was a child – and, like most kids, my favourite day was Saturday. You knew when you woke up if it was a Saturday because my mum started making soup really early in the morning. The smells wafting through the house were just delicious: the pumpkin and all the other vegetables going in, then the dumplings, and a little bit of beef shin and thyme. Lots of beautiful, delicious ingredients went into my mum's Saturday Soup, and she'd trill hymns and songs from musicals while she was making it. Down in the kitchen, she really was 'Maria' from *West Side Story*: she was living it, and she had a lovely voice so it was a pleasure to wake up and hear her downstairs, singing, '"Maria! I just met a girl . . ."'

Then she'd make us a typical Jamaican breakfast of ackee and salt fish with plantain, which the Queen apparently loves to eat whenever she goes to Jamaica. It's Her Majesty's favourite breakfast, no less, and a right royal treat wherever you are in the world, from Kingston to Kingstanding.

People would come and go all day long on a Saturday and it was really nice to connect with everyone. You had your 'aunties' and 'uncles' coming over, who were like family even if they weren't actual relatives: you had Auntie Vera, who was my mum's mate; you had Auntie Shirley, who was my godmother; and Uncle Percy, who was like a father figure to me. Uncle Percy was so cool, the friendliest guy ever. A big, fat, chirpy character with a moustache, who reminded me of Oliver Hardy from Laurel and Hardy, he smelt of cigarettes and chewed green Wrigley's spearmint gum. I wasn't allowed chewing gum and he used to give me a piece on the sly, so I loved it when he was around, and everyone else too. My mum made her Saturday Soup to keep everyone going throughout the day.

Sometimes Mum also made cockerel soup, using a stock that said 'Cock Soup' on the packet. When I was old enough – old enough to know better – I used to go round the table and say, 'Are you enjoying that? Do you like cock soup?'

Everyone said I was really cheeky for saying it, but I couldn't help it, because it made me laugh so much.

Mum gave incredible parties. The road would be packed with cars; the house would be full of people. All the furniture would be moved around to make space. Everybody arrived looking stylish. Auntie Shirley would be in a catsuit and platform heels and her husband, Mackie, with his Afro and thick moustache, bare-chested under his waistcoat with a medallion round his neck, used to look like he'd just come off stage at an Earth, Wind & Fire concert. This was the late seventies and early eighties and the music was mostly reggae, calypso and soul – as well as Abba, because my mum loved Abba. She had very eclectic taste in music.

The food would be immense, an English and Jamaican fusion of mutton and rice, Southern fried chicken, curried goat, plantain, rice and peas, fried dumpling and salt fish fritters – and Mum always, always served tiny sausages on cocktail sticks stuck all over a pineapple, her *Abigail's Party* flourish. It was a fabulous Jamlish spread and you wouldn't want to miss it.

Whole families would come, from the grandparents to the grandkids, and as the evening wore on, the children would go upstairs and fall asleep on Mum's bed under a big pile of coats. My brother and sister, being older than I was, were allowed to stay up a little bit later, but I would be sent to bed early on and I'd be gutted. Until, that is, I discovered that I could hear everything through the air vents on the wall in my bedroom. After that, I used to sit with my ear to them and listen to the party vibes.

There was always pure merriment and laughter at Mum's

parties. Auntie Shirley's laugh was so loud that you could hear it above the beats and Auntie Vera was just as noisy. They were young women in their prime, having a really great Saturday night – and my mum was at the centre of everything, spreading sunshine and joy among her guests.

Meanwhile, I'd fall asleep on the floor next to the air vents, trying my hardest not to miss a thing. I've always suffered with FOMO, which is fear of missing out.

Home

We lived in the kind of street where the kids played out every single day. It was always the same crew: there was Karen, who lived across the road; Samantha, the shy one; Sarah, who was lovely; and the Gafneys, a family of seven who lived in a three-bedroom house at the top of the road. It was a quiet street where nothing much ever happened – until the day that one of the younger Gafney brothers was attacked by a stray dog. I saw the whole thing happen: the dog took a massive chunk out of his leg and blood poured everywhere. I had to help him hobble back to his mum, screaming in pain, and for weeks afterwards the kids on our street never stopped talking about savage dogs and gushing wounds.

I was a lot shyer when I was a kid than I am now. I was the quiet one on our road. Although maybe my childhood friends from back then wouldn't agree with that . . . In fact, no, it's actually not true, now I think about it. I was out in the street from an early age doing cartwheels and acrobatics, so it's a total lie! But *in my heart* I think of myself as quite shy and retiring.

(I don't know what it is about putting a camera in front of me, but I absolutely love it and always want to be in shot – you may notice that, when picking up National Television Awards, there's always a competition between us as to who can get into the middle shot when Phil and Holly accept the award for the Most Popular Daytime Programme. Dr Ranj beat me to it once but it's usually me who wins that contest.)

Shy or not, I was always out on the street as a kid – I was your typical tomboy all through my childhood: I loved jeans and trousers and never wanted to wear a dress. The first dress I remember wearing was at my sister's wedding in 1985, along with a silly hat. I was so moody that day. I couldn't wait to take it off. I was influenced by the clothes my brother wore – and he'd been into the American sporty look ever since my mum had sent him on a trip to visit our Auntie Mavis in Florida when he was eleven and he'd come back wearing tube socks and speaking with an American accent.

I'd get my gear on – shorts, baseball cap, T-shirt, trainers – and go out and roller skate or pedal on my big-wheel go-kart; sometimes I'd pretend I was John McEnroe at Wimbledon and bang a ball up against people's houses. I'd scream, 'You cannot be serious!' in an American accent when the man at the corner house told me off and chased me: it was so scary but I loved it.

Our estate was built around a big hill called Pimple Hill, which people said was dangerous. I think they were talking about stranger danger, but we used to sneak along there anyway, of course. It was always really windy at the summit of the Pimple and you felt like you were on top of the world: I used to sing, dance and do cartwheels up there, or leap around pretending I was one of the Jets from *West Side Story*. On top of the Pimple you could become anything you wanted to be – and sometimes I'd just sit down and get lost in a dream as I stared out over the city. It was an amazing place to escape into your own thoughts, although in those days I was mostly thinking about sweets, comics and my first crush, Stephen, if I'm honest.

I was very close to my brother and sister growing up, and we're still tight now. There was quite a big age gap and I had a different dad from them, but our mum helped to nurture a very strong bond between us. A lot of people from blended families will know what I mean when I say that I don't see them as my half-brother and -sister. There's nothing 'half' about them. In my eyes, they are simply my brother and sister.

Of course there were times when they did my head in. Saundra was a loving, protective older sister, but we shared a room and sometimes got on each other's nerves. She was into poetry and playing the violin, so she had a serious side. For some reason she also used to put on 'beauty' face masks and chase me round the house saying, 'Kiss Auntie Saundra! Kiss Auntie Saundra!' which was absolutely terrifying.

People were always getting Saundra's name wrong, myself included. It's a Scottish version of Sandra and you say it *Sawndra*, but I used to call her Sandra as a kid. I mean, have you even heard of a Saundra? She was never a Saundra to me. She would correct other people if they called her Sandra, but she never corrected me in her life. I guess she loves me and lets me call her whatever I want to, because I'm her baby sister.

Our shared bedroom was quite a long room and our beds were at opposite ends – I was nearest the door and my sister was near the window – so it was almost like having our own rooms, because you felt you were in your own little area. We had drawers under our beds to keep our stuff in, so if we had anything to hide, that was where it went. (In my case, that was sweets and crisps, mainly!) All our possessions were under our beds, which helped Mum to keep the room tidy.

Our mum was incredibly house proud. You had to take your shoes off in the house. If Mum saw you walking around with your shoes on, her eyes wouldn't leave your feet – to the point where you'd feel uncomfortable and then you'd take your shoes off.

She absolutely loved antique furniture and had a collection of crystal wine glasses and blue and white Chinese plates that were arranged in a beautiful antique display cabinet. It was the biggest potential accident zone in the house and a source of true terror for me and Nicky, who were always getting into trouble for breaking things.

The day I put my foot through the bottom half of the cabinet is a day I won't forget.

I was in the middle of a fight with Nicky when I heard a sickening crunch as I stepped backwards. We both froze. 'Oh, no! Mum'll kill me!' I yelped.

'Don't worry, we'll fix it,' Nicky said, every bit as scared as I was.

He went outside, got some dirt, mixed it up with a little bit of glue and covered the hole with the dirt paste, which was pretty ingenious of him. It was a terrible job, but my mum didn't notice, thank goodness – and I don't think she ever found out about it.

There was a lot of role play in my family, a lot of messing around. We all had a bit of a theatrical flair. My brother and sister were both really talented musicians – Saundra was an amazing pianist and my brother was a brilliant drummer – and although I didn't play any instruments, I thought I was a great singer, even though I wasn't. When we had our own band, they'd say, 'Al, you can't sing,' and I'd say, 'I absolutely can sing and you know I can.'

As far as I was concerned, I was the most talented of the three of us, lol. I was absolutely destined for the job I do today.

It gave Mum a lot of pleasure to watch us singing, dancing and having a laugh. She positively encouraged us to show off, even if it was just entertaining her friends at home, with the broomstick as a microphone and a musical soundtrack on the record player. Nicky and Saundra knew every word of the Abba album *Arrival*; I knew all the songs and dances from *Annie*.

Mum took us to every musical or kids' show that came to Birmingham. We got dressed up in our best clothes and went to see shows like *Seven Brides for Seven Brothers*, *Oklahoma!* and *South Pacific*. Looking back, we were very lucky to have the opportunity, although I didn't always appreciate it at the time.

I'll never forget when the actress in *South Pacific* came on and started singing, 'I'm gonna wash that man right out of my hair,' I turned to Mum and said, 'This is rubbish. Can we go?'

'Absolutely not,' she said firmly. 'We are not going anywhere.'

I didn't try to argue. I never went against what Mum said. Like so many of her peers, who were also single parents, she was a mother and father in one. She was the head of the household and the breadwinner, and she administered the discipline. You just didn't mess with her.

Mum

My mum was really proud of who she was. She spent the first nine years of her life in Jamaica and held onto her little green Jamaican passport long after she moved to the UK. She was always saying that she was born 'under the clock' in Kingston. I never knew what it meant, but I'm told there's a clock tower at the main crossroads in Kingston, and if you're a true Kingstonian, you say you were born under it. Even though you weren't.

Mum didn't have an easy childhood. In 1954, when she was six, her mother Monica left Jamaica to go to England, leaving her in the care of her grandmother Beatrice. It was Beatrice who taught Mum to cook back in Jamaica, which was a blessing, because my great-grandmother definitely knew her way around the kitchen.

Monica went to Birmingham to live with Auntie Mavis, who was the matriarch of our family. Mavis was a district nurse in Mosley and helped a lot of her relatives come over to England or go to America. It was quite a big part of West Indian culture to help one another settle somewhere else, find a job and get established.

Mavis believed that you could achieve anything you wanted if you worked hard – and that lesson was passed down to my mum, who absorbed it early on. If you stayed with Mavis when you arrived from Jamaica, she taught you everything you needed to know about how to get on in 'the mother country'. She was very big on teaching etiquette: you didn't swear, you were house proud and you behaved with impeccable manners. You never, ever swore in front of Auntie Mavis – or Monica or my mum.

After three years apart, by which time Monica had met a new husband in Leeds and was pregnant with another child, my mum got the call to go and live with her mum. Mum was very sick on the boat over here – she ate nothing but biscuits for two weeks straight. When she arrived, aged nine, she was taken to her new home and put up in the attic to sleep. She used to say that she was like a modern-day Cinderella while she was living in that house. Her stepdad wouldn't let her call him Dad, which always made her feel like an outsider, and she had to do a lot of housework and chores.

At the age of fifteen, she came to Birmingham to live with her cousins Carmen and Gertie, under the guidance of her Aunt May. She started her life from scratch again. In 1965, she met a young Jamaican man and became pregnant with Saundra, who was born in 1966. In those days, people disapproved if you weren't married when you were having a baby, so when Mum was five months pregnant with my brother, Nicholas, they quickly tied the knot. Nicky was born in 1967 and the young couple rented rooms here and there until they landed a council flat on the ninth floor of the tower block in Nechells, my first home.

Unfortunately, the marriage didn't work out and by the

early 1970s, Mum was a single mother, juggling two or three jobs at a time. She was always a grafter and did whatever she could to keep her family going: she was a barmaid, a cashier in a casino, a Tupperware manager, an usherette, a film and TV extra, an auxiliary nurse and a reservations clerk for Horizon Tours, among other things. She worked so, so hard to make a better life for herself and her children and we never wanted for anything. If my sister wanted a doll's house, she had a doll's house. If Nicky wanted a drum set or a new suit, she'd get it for him. I had my roller skates, go-kart and tennis racket all because my mum was juggling so many jobs.

If there were times when Mum struggled to put food on the table, she didn't show it. I remember there was always something home-cooked on the side of the stove. 'Don't touch it until I come home,' she'd warn, but while she was out and about, I would be a little bit cheeky, go into the pot and have a taste. Then I'd have another taste, and another.

'Who's been eating the food?' she'd ask, when she got in. 'A quarter of the dish is gone!'

'Not me!' I'd say. 'It must have been Saundra and Nicky.'

'Really?' she'd say, smiling wryly and giving me a knowing look.

My mum's cooking was so good that I just could not stay away, especially if she'd made her brown chicken and rice. It was such a simple, delicious dish: she'd cook the meat down into a beautiful gravy with onions, peppers and garlic, and serve it on a bed of white basmati rice; I still make it exactly the same way she did.

Her corned-beef rice was also irresistible. She'd cook onion and pepper, with a little bit of all-purpose seasoning and some Worcestershire sauce, then add tomatoes, a little thyme and a can of corned beef. Now, corned beef was once considered a poor man's food – and maybe it still is – but I eat this dish to this day and it's so nice! It is one of the most comforting dishes ever, and if you have it with mashed potato instead of rice, it's heaven on a plate. Try it: mashed potato and corned beef. YUM.

It must have been tough for Mum working all the hours she worked but she just got on with it. One of the downsides was having to leave her kids at home, and a lot of my early memories are of sitting in the top room of our house, looking out of the window, waiting for her. I was obsessed with my mum. I couldn't wait for her to get home. Sometimes I sat there for hours, just waiting and waiting. 'When will she be here?' I'd fret. 'When?'

My heart would leap when she finally arrived. 'Oo-ooh!' she'd call out, when she came through the door. It was her native call, her version of 'Cooey!' If one of us got lost when we went shopping, I'd hear her call, 'Oo-ooh!' and I'd call back, 'Oo-ooh!' and then we'd find each other.

What's funny is that my son has picked up the habit of saying, 'Oo-ooh!' when he comes in, which always reminds me of Mum and makes me smile. I like the way certain mannerisms pass down through generations: it makes me wonder if Aidan's kids and grandkids will one day be saying, 'Oo-ooh!' too, sweetly echoing my lovely mum's call.

Dad

Mum met my dad, Clifford Hammond, at a casino in Birmingham, where she was working as a cashier. She changed his chips for him when he won at gambling one night in 1974.

'And this is for you,' Cliff said, giving her a red chip worth fifty pounds.

'Oh, thank you!' my mum said, taken aback. Fifty pounds was a real lot of money in those days.

Cliff asked her if she'd like to meet up with him sometime. She said yes and he came and picked her up in his beautiful Jaguar, like some modern-day Prince Charming.

Cliff was a big man with a big presence. He was very charismatic, the life and soul of the party, and people were captivated by him. He loved Elvis and wore gold chains around his neck – thick gold chains, not little diddly bits – crisply pressed, open-necked shirts and bracelets studded with diamonds.

Cliff really wooed my mum and she fell madly in love with him. I think she was partly seduced by his lifestyle: he had nice cars and knew a lot of famous people.

Initially she didn't know he was married. Then one day he brought his daughter along to meet my brother and sister and laid out the real situation. By that point, though, it was too late to change the course of Fate, as Mum was pregnant with me. She had prayed to have Cliff's baby. Now I was on my way.

It was messed up, but Mum made the best of it. And it must have been in the stars – otherwise you wouldn't be reading this book, would you, babs?

My mum treated me a little bit differently from my brother and sister growing up, if I'm honest. I think she felt she had to give me more love and attention, because I didn't have my dad around as much as they did, and she felt guilty that I was illegitimate. She had been married to Saundra and Nicky's dad, who was now remarried and had another family, but I was a love child.

Sometimes she maybe went a bit too far the other way, to the point where it was a little bit embarrassing. She would put me first. She would give me more. If I asked for something, I would get it. I'd hate to think that my brother or sister ever felt lesser or not as important, because I believe she loved them just as much as she loved me. She was just trying to compensate for my absent dad.

One of my dad's businesses was importing trucks to Jamaica from England, so he was often travelling back and forth between the two countries. He bought and sold farm machinery and was involved with Pat Roach, the scrapyard millionaire, wrestler and actor, who used to come over to our house sometimes. Pat Roach was officially the strongest man in Great Britain for years and played villains in the Indiana Jones films, *Conan the Destroyer*, *Clash of the Titans* and the James Bond film *Never Say Never Again*; he also played 'Bomber' in the TV series *Auf Wiedersehen, Pet*. He and my dad had a lot in common: they were both very driven and ambitious and enjoyed doing business together.

My dad's favourite programme was the US soap *Dallas*. His dream was to be a farmer with a ranch, his own guns, land and cattle; he wanted to be the Jamaican JR and everything he did was building up to buying that ranch. To be fair, I loved *Dallas* too. We only had one television, so we would all gather around the TV in the living room and watch it together. I always felt a thrill when I heard the *Dallas* theme tune start because me, Saundra and Nicky would stand up and start dancing to it. 'Der, der-der, de der-de-de der-der, der der der de-de derrr!' My mum used to laugh, because we did it every single time *Dallas* came on.

Dad came to our house sporadically. He'd just land on us and expect the whole world to stop for him – and because my mum was in love with him, the whole world did stop. No matter what I was doing, if my dad turned up at my house, I wasn't doing it any more: I had to come down and be in his presence. It was all about Clifford. It was his show now and we all had to give him our attention.

Suddenly, it would be like he'd been there for ever. Sometimes I'd be happy to see him. Oh, it's so lovely to have my mum and dad together, I'd think. Other times, I'd be secretly thinking, This is not normal. He goes away, he comes back. Yes, he's my dad but I don't really know him. I often wished my mum would marry Uncle Percy.

Occasionally, Dad used to bring along his other children, my brother and sister on his side. He'd just turn up with them. He wanted everyone to get on nicely, regardless of who their parents were, and my mum was fine with that.

My dad went on to have another two children with different women and, out of all of them, I resembled him the most. He could never have gone to court and said that I wasn't his child, because everyone would have started laughing. 'Yeah, right, then. Whatever. Dismissed!'

Even Dad couldn't believe how alike we were. He'd put his hands next to mine and say, 'Look, even our hands are the same!' That's probably another reason why my mum loved me so much – because I reminded her of the love of her life.

Three of Cliff's children have Ali in their name somewhere – Ali, Alyssa and Alison – because my dad and Muhammad Ali were friends. At least, every time Muhammad Ali came to England, he would call up my dad to be his bodyguard. I've got pictures of Ali and my dad together at different events in Birmingham, and you know what? There's a real resemblance. They look like they could be brothers.

I met Muhammad Ali about three times during my childhood. There are photos of him kissing and hugging me, my mum and dad looking on and loving it. You can see in the photos that I just want to get away, though. I was only little at the time and didn't want any old person giving me a great big bear hug!

I wasn't interested in Ali's fame or fortune, but I do remember him showing me some great magic tricks. He even gave me my own little magic trick to take home with me: a tiny traffic light with red, amber and green sensors;

when you passed your hand over it, the lights would change to all-green or all-red. To me, aged five or six, it was really magic. I'm glad I was named after him.

I looked like my dad physically, but we weren't alike in character, except in one obvious way: Dad liked showing off and singing Elvis songs and I think he would have loved to be on television. Unfortunately he didn't pass his lovely voice on to me, and neither did my mum. Yes, I've finally accepted that mine's not the best of voices, as you'll know if you've heard me sing a duet with Michael Bublé. (But I still say that no one can touch my karaoke version of 'Mustang Sally'.)

My dad definitely had the lifestyle. Whenever we went out for a meal with him, he always paid. 'Have anything you want,' he'd say. He introduced us to Chinese food back when it was a luxury to have a Chinese takeaway. We had it every time he came and I became obsessed with it, to the point where I asked my mum, 'Do you think Santa will bring me some Chinese food for breakfast, if I write and ask him?'

I didn't realize how amazing Santa actually was until that year when he delivered me a cold Chinese meal – RESULT!

I still love Chinese food today. In fact, whenever I'm giving directions, instead of using pubs as landmarks – 'Turn left at the Red Lion and right at the Bull's Head' – I use Chinese restaurants as my landmarks, because I know them all. So I give directions like, 'Turn left at Yat Wa and right at Jade City . . .'

My dad could be a little bit intimidating, at times. There was a National Front presence in Kingstanding, where we lived, and my brother remembers a day when a boy said something really racist to him as he and Saundra were walking back from school. When Nicky came home and told my mum, my dad happened to be there, and even though they weren't his children, my dad marched him and Saundra up to this boy's house. 'You see these two kids?' he bellowed. 'Don't ever speak to them like that again. If you see them, ignore them, or you'll have me to deal with.'

They never had any trouble again.

I wasn't scared of my dad. Maybe the word is respect – I respected him and used to pander to him. I remember playing in the house with my best friend Emma once, when my mum had gone off to work. Suddenly my dad arrived. 'Oh, my God, my dad's here!' I told Emma. 'Go upstairs.'

Bearing in mind that my dad didn't live in our house, why was I so fearful of him telling me off that I made my friend go upstairs and hide so that he didn't see her? She hid for the whole hour that he was there. It was only when he left that I rushed upstairs and told her, 'You can come out now, babes.'

One day, he came straight to our house from the airport, after flying in from Jamaica. 'See these boots?' he said, grinning down at his feet. 'These are the most expensive pair of snakeskin boots in the world.'

'Why are they so expensive?' my mum asked.

He bent down, unzipped a boot and a load of ganja fell out.

That was my dad! Cliff was charismatic and charming, but he was naughty: he'd illegally bring drugs into the country in the days when people could get away with it, before

29

they introduced sniffer dogs and body scans at the airport. I'm embarrassed to admit it, because I've never been remotely interested in drugs, but I remember him coming to our house and giving my mum a roll of money – and, thinking about it now, it was probably money earned from smuggling ganja. So shady.

When I was about ten, he emigrated to Jamaica and I didn't see much of him after that until my mum took me out there when I was sixteen, by which time he'd bought his land and his ranch and was exactly where he'd always wanted to be. He was like a king when we visited him in Jamaica. You could tell by the way people spoke about him that he was respected and feared in the community: they called him Mr Hammond and you could see the unease in their eyes when they spoke to him. I'm not surprised, either, because he drove everywhere with a massive shotgun tucked under his pick-up truck. He didn't mess around.

Me and Mum stayed in a hotel and my dad used to collect us most days and take us out and about. I'd sit in the back of the truck, and Mum and Dad would be up front. Imagine this little girl from Birmingham, bumping along dusty roads in her dad's truck with a shotgun underneath it. What the heck is going on here? I kept thinking.

Wherever we stopped, people would say, 'Hello, Mr Hammond,' and Dad would gesture to me and say, 'Guess who this is?'

They'd size me up for a moment. 'Oh, it's got to be your daughter.'

'Yes, my daughter, so beautiful!'

Dad seemed to like showing me off, but I felt it was just

pleasantries. If you're so proud of me, why have you not been around for me? I thought. Where have you been all this time?

Meanwhile, you could see that my mum just adored him. She thought he was incredible, charming and funny – she found him absolutely hilarious. Love is blind, as they say!

I actually got on a lot better with Dad's brother, my Uncle Paul, who owned a fleet of buses and taxis out in Jamaica. Uncle Paul was more grounded than my dad and seemed to want to know who the real Alison was, rather than just talking surface chit-chat. He was kind and nice and just more fun to be with than my dad.

After a while, I could see my dad starting to get jealous of Uncle Paul, though. 'Oh, no, you're not spending any time with Paul today. You're with me,' he'd say.

One day, Dad took me to see his ranch. He parked up on a hill, put his arm around me and pointed at the lush vegetation that stretched out in front of us. 'You see that?' he said. 'One day, darling, all of this will be yours, as far as the eye can see.'

I'll never forget that little speech. It was so dramatic, like something out of *The Lion King*. Still, he was telling the truth, because when he died last year, he left the ranch to his five children.

There was a little lamb in the truck with me on our way back from the ranch. It was the sweetest little lamb and I really connected with it on the journey.

'It's not a lamb, it's a kid goat,' my dad said, when I told him how cute I thought it was.

That evening, when we sat down to a big dinner with

Dad's friends and family, I asked my uncle, 'Where's the baby goat gone?'

He pointed at the joint on the table. 'There. We're having it in honour of your visit.'

I felt ever so guilty! That little goat had lost his life for me and I couldn't eat any of it. 'Ah, I'll pass, if that's okay,' I said.

I've never eaten goat from that day.

As for my dad, now that I'm an adult I don't hold any grudges towards him for not being around much when I was a child. He did the best he could do at the time. That's what I have to remember and respect. He was the only dad he could be – he couldn't be anything other than who he was – and my mum loved him. Every single one of us is individual and unique, and that includes our parents. Rest in peace, Dad.

So there you have a few snapshots from my early life and background to give a sense of who I was as a kid and what kind of family I came from. It wasn't exactly normal, but it was full of love, people, mischief and food, and I wouldn't have had it any other way.

2. MY MUM AND ME

My mum is the reason I am who I am. She was the best mum ever and the love she gave me was unbelievable. Mum was at the centre of all the good things that happened to me and helped me in so many ways: she loved me, guided me, protected me, inspired me and made me laugh – and, somehow or other, she always saved the day.

I never had to worry about anything, because I had my mum. She made me feel safe and that everything was going to be all right. She could calm any situation with just a few words, and if I was angry or upset, she could instantly make me feel better.

Here are a few memories of Maria to give you a sense of just how lucky I was to be her daughter.

Screen debut

The moment you first turn it on for the cameras has to count as significant in the life of a TV presenter – and, like most things in my life, I have my mum to thank for giving me the chance to discover it.

She was fascinated by everything to do with showbiz. I'd say, 'Mum, it's really not all that,' but she wouldn't listen. She loved celebrities and the whole shebang. So I guess it's in my blood in a way.

Mum was so proud that her daughter was on television. She'd phone people to say, 'Alison's on TV now! Put the TV on.'

She watched everything I did, so I would always phone her after I'd filmed something and ask, 'How was it?'

'Al, it was brilliant!' she'd say.

My son would pipe up in the background: 'Mum, I saw you make a mistake!'

'No, it was fine,' my mum would reassure me. 'No one would have noticed.'

She was always there to say, 'You were great, Alison.'

You've never seen anyone get so much joy out of her daughter. It made her happy to see me having a good time and it was the same with my son: she got so much joy out of her grandson! He was everything to her – he couldn't put a foot wrong. If we went to see her and I was complaining, 'Mum, he's been ever so naughty today,' she'd say, 'Oh, no, don't be silly! He's lovely. He's wonderful.'

My mum saw us through rose-tinted glasses. We were just perfect in her eyes, and luckily for her, we were perfect – lol.

I think it would be difficult not to have a positive attitude to life if you had a mum like mine. Her dream was to be in television, and when I was growing up she worked as an extra in TV programmes like *Empire Road* and *Angels*, as well as a film called *Marjorie and the Preacherman*. She did so much, my mum – she literally furnished our home by being an extra in TV shows. My brother was forever waiting around for her at the Pebble Mill Studios in Edgbaston, Birmingham, during the school holidays, until eventually he started doing walk-on parts as well.

In all the years she worked in TV, Mum only ever had a single line to say: 'It's water under the bridge.'

Me and Nicky suddenly remembered it the other day. It was the anniversary of our mum's death and we went and sat by her grave – I call it her 'for-ever bed'. As we were talking about how much we miss Mum, we started laughing about how we used to tease her with her one line of dialogue whenever we got into trouble. She'd be telling us off about something and we'd turn to her and say, 'Mum, it's water under the bridge.' It really used to tickle us – and then she'd laugh and stop telling us off, so it was pretty useful too.

It was thanks to my mum that I made my TV debut,

forty years ago, when I was six years old. Mum was cast in a non-speaking role in a TV movie called *Artemis 81*, playing the mum in a family of four. When she found out that they still hadn't cast the rest of her character's family, she jumped in and said, 'My son's an actor and my daughter's an actress, so why not use them?'

We weren't actors, we were my mum's children and didn't have a bloody clue about acting – but since we just had to be ourselves in front of a camera, it wasn't very hard. And we got paid for it too.

So that was how Mum got me and my brother into a full-length feature film starring Hywel Bennett and Daniel Day-Lewis. I was six and played a six-year-old; Nicky was fourteen and played a fourteen-year-old. Another actor played our dad. You can watch *Artemis 81* on YouTube if you've got a few spare hours and literally nothing else to do. We're the only Black family in it, so you won't miss us.

We went to Denmark to do the filming and the producers really looked after us. They took us on the ferry and gave us money for the slot machines and Space Invaders. We had a whale of a time, all expenses paid; it was like a family trip to Denmark with a random dad. And it was brilliant for Mum, because she could have us with her while she was working.

Guess who else is in the film? None other than Sting. Sting is in this film! He plays an angel. I'm not going to lie, though: it's probably one of the worst films I've ever seen. It's crap.

In the movie, our onscreen family commits suicide in a car. We park in a garage, keep the engine going and kill ourselves with carbon monoxide. *Oh, happy day!* We've got no speaking role. We're just, like, this family who die in a car and get taken off in an ambulance.

Whoops! Spoiler alert! I'm so, so sorry if I've ruined it for you. Never mind, you can just doze off while you watch it now.

Later, you see the four of us in a grave, pretending to be dead. I remember the director saying, 'Okay, everyone, hold your breath. And action!'

We lay down, held our breath and pretended to be dead. It's hard to believe I was only six, because I can actually remember turning it on for the cameras.

'Okay, and cut! Everybody relax,' the director said.

So that was my first ever job in TV – playing someone who'd died. When I watched it, I thought, Wow, Mum, did you really get us to do this? What kind of mother are you? Lol.

Holidays

My mum had a beautiful speaking voice, so soft and gentle. You'd just fall into a trance when you heard her speak. She didn't sound like a Brummie, like I do. In fact, if you didn't know my mum, she'd speak to you in quite a posh English accent.

She had a very lovely telephone voice. People who used to phone for me would say, 'Who was that on the phone?'

'It was my mum.'

'Wow, she doesn't sound anything like you, Alison!'

It was only when my mum knew you well and was happy in your company that she'd soften the tones and you'd hear a Jamaican twang just slightly seep in – and that would be the indicator that she was comfortable in your presence.

My mum's beautiful speaking voice got her a long way in life. Literally. She was so good at her job as telephone reservations clerk at Horizon Travel – basically, booking people's holidays for them when they rang up – that she was always being given free trips and holidays as a bonus. And when they weren't free, she'd get a major discount.

She often turned them down. 'They've offered me a trip to Paris but we can't go because it's during term time,' she'd say.

'Come on, Mum, please!' I'd beg her.

'No,' she'd say.

Occasionally, she'd relent and take us out of school, and off we'd go to Paris or Mallorca for three days' holiday. We were really lucky. We could travel at a time when most people couldn't afford to go abroad, back in the days when you'd get on a plane and see people smoking cigarettes in the seats at the back. It's weird to think of it now: people actually used to smoke on planes. Every seat had an ashtray, and when the no-smoking light went off, puffs of smoke would waft forward to where we were sitting at the front.

We went to Malta a couple of times. My mum made friends wherever she went and we met some lovely people out in Malta, including a very sweet lady we used to call 'Nana Nina'. One evening, Nana Nina invited us to her house for dinner. Now, snails were on the menu and she put them all in a big pot on the hob, ready to be cooked. We went out for a walk and when we came back, all the snails were climbing out of the pot and up the wall. It was like a horror movie: there were snails and slime trails literally all the way up to the ceiling. It was disgusting.

It put me off eating snails for life. Even if you sautéd them in the most delicious combination of parsley butter, garlic and shallots, and baked them with a sprinkle of brioche croutons, I just couldn't. Never. No way. Not having it, because it would still be a mouthful of slime. YUK!

Auntie Mavis

One of the most important people in my mum's life was her cousin, Auntie Mavis. Mum really looked up to Auntie Mavis, who had left Jamaica for England in the 1950s and had gone on to help many of her relatives to do the same. Auntie Mavis was very highly thought of in our family: when you heard people talking about her, you knew they were speaking about someone special. She was a pioneering, strong, religious woman who had done very well in life: she had gone from Jamaica to Birmingham and now owned a care-home business in Fort Lauderdale, Florida, where she lived in a beautiful bungalow.

Whenever she came to England, Auntie Mavis would have her own room in my mum's house. We still to this day call the spare room in Mum's house 'Auntie Mavis's room'. I was eight years old when we first went to visit her in Florida, for Christmas, and the trip is still vivid in my memory, partly because, from the moment we landed, my mum suddenly started speaking in an American accent. I don't know why she did this – just for fun, maybe – but, of course, I copied her. So we both spoke in American accents while we were staying with Auntie Mavis.

We arrived in Fort Lauderdale on Christmas Eve. Auntie

Mavis pulled out all the stops and put on a massive pork dinner for us, although by then I think I was too tired to appreciate it. She was amazing and generous and took care of us in every way during our stay: she took us shopping and on day trips – she really spoilt us.

Every night I'd go into her bedroom and she'd read the Bible to me. She had a very strong faith and explained all the stories beautifully, so I found them really interesting.

'Always have your Bible with you,' she used to say to me.

And, you know, I do always have a Bible with me – although, to be fair, I need to read it more often. Reading the Bible makes me feel safer and more secure in myself. A lot of people don't like the idea of it, but you don't necessarily have to be religious to read it. Take Proverbs, for instance. I like reading Proverbs because it's full of wisdom that you can apply to your everyday life.

My mum sent me, Nicky and Saundra to Sunday school every week and in later years she gave me the Bible that Auntie Mavis had given her decades earlier. 'In life, you need your own satnav,' Mum told me, 'and the satnav I'm going to give you, Alison, is this Bible.'

Americana

Mum spoke with an American accent whenever she saw any of her American family, so it was something that seemed completely normal to me, until I got into trouble for it. To be fair, though, it wasn't sounding American that got me into hot water exactly – it was what I actually said . . .

Our trip to Florida when I was eight had kicked off a love of all things American in me, just as it had for my brother when he was eleven. American jeans, American football, American music – we loved them all. Even my sister Saundra wanted to get on the American bandwagon. Years later, in 1998, I suddenly found myself becoming a birthing partner when my sister was having my beautiful niece, Jasmine. I only went to the hospital to say hello; the next thing I knew I was holding gas and air and patting my sister's forehead while occasionally screaming, 'PUSH!'

The midwife, Adèle, and my brother-in-law, Andy, were great additions to the team. I just love that my sister wanted me in the room. Every time she had a contraction, she would burst into this American accent: 'I need *waaa*der! Gimme some *waaa*der.'

Literally as soon as the contraction finished she was

back to her normal accent. Andy and I were just creasing the whole time. Even Adèle asked if we were American. (Can you guess what Jasmine's middle name was? Yes, she's Jasmine *Adèle* – my sister did the same as my mother did with me and named her after the midwife.)

I was probably the first person to see my niece, which is up there as one of the most incredible moments in my life – to witness an actual birth!

A couple of years after the trip to Florida, I got myself into a situation one day on my way home from school, when I noticed some Mormons up ahead of me, knocking on doors. They looked really well turned out and were speaking with American accents, so I struck up a conversation with them in my stupid American accent.

Just for fun, I told them I was from Florida and had moved to the UK with my mum, ten years earlier.

'Why don't we come to your house and give you and your mom a presentation about what it means to be a Mormon?' they suggested.

'Yeah, come over!' I said, and as I was saying it, I was thinking, Give them a fake address, Alison, give them a fake address.

But as the words came out, I found myself saying my correct address, 'Forty-six Beckenham Avenue,' and thinking, Oh, no, what am I doing?

'We'll try to come tomorrow after school,' they said. 'Is that a good time?'

'Sure, no problem,' I said. 'My mom's going to love meeting you. Obviously, she's from America and you guys are from America, so it's gonna be great.'

We said goodbye and I went home. Oh dear, I thought, I need to tell my mum what I've done.

She was in the kitchen making tea when I got in. 'Er, Mum, I've got some Mormons coming tomorrow,' I said.

'Why?' she asked.

'I've just seen them on the street and I gave them my address. Are you okay speaking to them?'

'Yes, no problem.'

'There's one thing, though, Mum. I told them I was from America and that we moved here ten years ago. Can you back me up?'

She tutted disapprovingly. 'Oh, Alison! I'm not lying for you, if that's what you're asking.'

'It's not about lying!' I said, panic rising, 'but I'm going to look so stupid when they come, because I've told them I'm American and you are too.'

'Well, I'm not speaking in an American accent to them. It's not going to happen.'

'Mum, please!' I begged.

'I'm not doing it. Go upstairs,' she said crossly.

I came home from school the next day dreading the arrival of the Mormons. This is going to be so embarrassing, I thought. They're going to find me out! They're going to realize I'm not really American.

I hid upstairs.

At four o'clock, the knock came on the door. I crouched on the landing, straining to listen, absolutely cringing.

Mum opened the door and I heard her say, 'Hi, how are you doing?'

In. Her. Best. American. Accent.

I couldn't believe it. It was the most convincing American accent ever.

'You know, we came to England ten years ago and we're so happy to be in Birming-HAM,' she said breezily. 'But we're really not interested in becoming Mormons; I'm sorry my daughter gave you the wrong impression. Thank you for calling. Bye!'

How nice it was of my mum to go against her core values and lie for me like that! Although she was angry with me, she understood that I'd got carried away and loved me too much to make me look stupid. I was so grateful to her.

Turkey talk

Christmas was always a really special time for our family, especially because of the food. My mum absolutely loved cooking Christmas lunch for everyone. Her roasts were legendary – and at Christmas she took things to another level. Mum's turkey had all the trimmings and much, much more. Her gravy! Her stuffing! Out. Of. This. World.

But one Christmas, Mum went off to Jamaica to meet up with my dad and left me, my brother and sister at home together. I know! When we look back, we can't believe our mum just left us! Although, admittedly, it was for two of the great loves of her life: Jamaica and my dad.

While Mum was gone, my sister was in charge; Saundra was eighteen at the time and looked after us for two weeks over the Christmas period.

She cooked a delicious dinner on Christmas Day, but everything felt a bit strange. When my brother put the turkey on the table, I said, 'Are you going to carve it?'

'No, we don't need to carve it,' he said. 'Mum's not here.' He broke off a leg and plonked it on my plate. 'Just bless it and eat it,' he said, and who was I to argue? Carved or not, it was delicious.

Because I was the youngest in the family, the others

always saw me as the baby who needed looking after – to the extent that Mum used to cook my Christmas turkey for me even when I was an adult. I know, it's a bit embarrassing but, hey-ho, that's life! So I was really touched when my sister offered to cook my turkey for me in 2020, our first Christmas without our mum. 'I'll do it this year,' she said. 'I'll do what Mum used to do.'

It was such a kind offer. 'Oh, sis, you're so gorgeous,' I said, 'but I think it's about time I grew up now.'

So I got my turkey and everything else I needed for our Christmas dinner. I was all prepared, and as I was getting into bed on Christmas Eve, I remembered that Mum had always woken up at five o'clock on Christmas morning to put the turkey into the oven. She liked to cook it for longer on a low heat so that it kept all its juices.

There's no way I'm waking up at five o'clock! I thought, with a chuckle. I'll just put it on at nine o'clock and it'll be ready by one.

Lo and behold, guess what time I woke up on Christmas morning? Five o'clock! That's my mum waking me up to go and put the turkey on, I thought.

I went downstairs, took the turkey out of the shed, where I'd left it seasoned the night before, and put it into the oven on a really low heat. As I was making the gravy and all the trimmings, I could almost feel my mum at my shoulder, guiding me.

Honestly, that turkey came out so good, and the gravy was absolutely bang on. I sat and ate it with my mum's picture next to me. Everyone gave me a round of applause at the end, because it was a fantastic meal. I won't say it was better than my mum's, but it was close, and my brother said it was the best turkey he'd ever tasted in his entire life.

I've finally grown up. I'm an adult. I've made my own Christmas lunch, I thought.

Thank you, Mum.

School

My mum always had her fingers in a lot of different pies. Along with her Horizon job, she got involved in Tupperware sales and did really, really well. I can always remember the house, packed with boxes everywhere, orders upon orders upon orders, which Nicky and Saundra used to help pack up. It was obvious my mum was very successful because to get to the bathroom you had to climb over so many boxes! She was a brilliant saleswoman and won prizes and bonuses galore, including a new car and a trip to Disney World. She went right to the top of the tree and became an area manager, with lots of people working under her.

All that grafting meant she missed out on the things that other mums who stayed at home did, like reading with her children. She didn't notice that my schoolwork wasn't up to scratch because she was juggling so many jobs. And since she wasn't on my education with regard to my reading, it wasn't until I was eleven that we realized I needed glasses.

One day, I was sitting at the back of the class and the teacher said, 'Can you actually see the board from there?'

'No, I can't,' I admitted.

My mum took me to have my eyes tested. With my new glasses, I could finally see the board and get on with my schoolwork. I instantly started reading and writing better and working so much harder. I could actually see!

School sports were my thing and it made me quite popular, so I enjoyed my school days. I loved hockey, basketball, sprinting, rounders, swimming and netball, and I played football with the boys. Mum wanted her children to have every possible chance in life and we did all kinds of extra activities after school, including music and dance. She signed me up to do acrobatics early on and I learnt to do the splits, as well as a front and backward walkover. I also went to dance classes and passed all my tap dancing and ballet grades. I can still do the splits today if I warm up properly with a bit of yoga and I dance all the time: in the kitchen, when I wake up, before I go to bed. I'm a natural mover.

I had a lovely group of girlfriends at school: Miranda, Louise, Debbie and Lorraine. We're still close and speak on the phone: one's a social worker, another works for the NHS; a couple are mums. What's great about your really old friends is that they know who you are and where you've come from. They've been there from the beginning and I can just be myself with them, which counts for a lot.

So, the girls in my class were really nice. It was the boys who could be mean. Occasionally they thought it was hilarious to comment on my weight. They didn't do it very often, though, and only when they were in a group, because I'd always come back with a funny retort and make them look stupid. And I could be quite self-deprecating, in a humorous way. I said it first – I suppose it was a defence mechanism – and I probably still do that a little bit to this day.

The girls never said anything nasty. We all took showers

together and I could see that my boobs were a lot bigger than the others' were, but if anything, they were envious. They were like, 'Wow, you've got lovely boobs!'

When I look back at photos of when I was younger, I think I look really slim, but everyone used to say that I was big for my age. 'Big-boned,' they said.

Did that mean I had a fat skeleton? I wondered.

'Are my bones fat?' I asked my mum.

'You're beautiful in every way,' she said, which was her answer to most of my questions, to be fair.

I always had it in my head that I was bigger than everyone else, but actually I look really normal in the pictures. If only I could be the size I was when my younger self thought I was fat! If I could be that size now, I'd be perfect.

Even more perfect than I already am!

Years later, when I went for a chest X-ray at my local hospital, they couldn't fit my shoulders into the image. 'You could never be really tiny because your natural bone structure is quite broad,' the radiographer told me.

'You mean, I'm naturally a big girl?'

She nodded. 'It's in your genes.'

It's the way I was made and you can't argue with biology, can you? I was destined to take up a little bit of extra space in the world: it's in my DNA. Which stands for deoxyribonucleic acid, by the way. I used to love biology.

My favourite teacher at school was Miss Colman, who taught science, and she was just amazing. Miss Colman was strict – she'd let you know about yourself if you got out of line or you were rude – but she was able to control the class in ways that I've never seen any other teacher do:

she'd give us one look and we knew we were pushing it. We respected Miss Colman and she respected us back; she was funny and she'd also laugh at our jokes. She was spot on as a teacher and engaged us because she got the balance completely right between strictness and making the class interesting. She made you want to learn the periodic table off by heart – and I did.

Miss Colman was also head of year and ran a tuck shop out of her office. In years ten and eleven, she asked me to be the tuck-shop monitor, so I'd go to her office two days a week, open her window into the playground and sell sweets from it. It was brilliant. I felt great that I was trusted to do that – to handle money and count it up – and later she made me a prefect, which did a lot for my confidence. I went on to do biology A level but I didn't get on with the teacher, so I pulled out, which just shows how important teachers are in our lives. Who knows? If I'd had someone else, I might have ended up a scientist!

When people ask me if I was bullied as a child I would say no, as the boys' behaviour towards me at school wasn't consistent and I felt that I could absolutely stand my ground. Looking back, I'm sure that my mum's unshakeable love gave me the strength and confidence to believe in and stick up for myself. What I did hate, though, was seeing other people being bullied and I would always have to say something, because it just didn't seem fair.

'Do you feel better about yourself when you make other people feel bad about themselves?' I'd ask the bullies. 'Wow, how cool are you?'

I could never keep my mouth shut, because I had this

sense that I was doing what was right. Then I would become the target of the attention, but I would just brush it off.

These days, I think the wise thing to do is to walk away when you're targeted. I've noticed that it really winds people up if you turn your back, or if you're silent, at a moment when they're trying to have an argument with you, because they're left having a full-on argument with themselves.

It's difficult to be silent when you've got something to say. But you don't need to say anything – you really don't – and your silence becomes powerful. Saying nothing is the wisest and most sensible thing to do, which is probably why I don't really get into conflict with people. Being silent gives you power to see what is going on.

The loudest person is usually the dumbest (only my opinion!) – and I know I'm quite loud sometimes, but you'll also notice a stillness within me, if you watch me. I'm quite observant and I listen to what people say: what they're saying normally tells me something about them. I'm listening to how they feel about themselves.

So if someone's saying, 'I hate you, Alison!' and they start to list the reasons why, I'll know that these are the things they hate about themselves and are projecting onto me. That's why, when I'm being trolled online, I have an off switch and I don't react. Silence is always the best response, I find. However, I sometimes can't help myself.

I wish I'd had the sense to say nothing the day I clashed with a boy called Junior in our Spanish class, though. I can't remember the lead-up to it now, but he called me a 'fat elephant' and it really did my head in. I hated being called an elephant by the boys at school. 'Oh, I didn't realize elephants were brown,' they'd say, as a little dig about my weight. Why are fat people always called elephants? I mean, elephants are large, but they're really not fat: they're muscly and they can run really fast.

When I came back with a retort and everybody started laughing – I think I called him 'an uneducated pig' in Spanish – Junior was so embarrassed that he punched me in the face. He literally boxed me in my face and sent my glasses flying right across the classroom, from one side to the other. In Jamaica, we call that a 'tump', and it really was a tump and a half. I saw stars – swear to God. I absolutely saw stars. What was even more unfair was that Junior didn't get into trouble for punching me. The Spanish teacher didn't do anything about it. Can you believe it?

When the lesson was over, all the boys were saying, 'That was well out of order. You can't have him punching you like that. You need to call him out.'

Before I knew it, the whole class had arranged for me and Junior to have a fight after school. 'I don't want to have a fight,' I kept saying.

'No, you've got to,' they insisted.

Soon everyone knew that Alison and Junior were going to have a fight after school on the green. I was mortified, but accepted that I had to go through with it. I'd never had a fight in my life, but this fight had been arranged and I couldn't not go.

It got to the end of the day and, oh, my God, I was going to have to fight now. I'm going to die, I thought.

I would normally walk home from school, but I think my mum must have had a sixth sense that I needed her that day. She never usually picked me up, but as I was coming through the gates she suddenly rocked up in her convertible XR3 injection with the roof down, and said, 'I just thought I'd pick you up today.'

I beamed at her. 'Ah, Mum, thank you!'

She literally saved me that day. Something in her gut had told her to pick me up from school and, since I didn't have to walk home, the fight didn't happen. I just got into my mum's car and sped off.

Sometimes Maria was my angel, other times my rock; either way, she was always amazing. She made me the person I am today and I'm so grateful to have had her for my mum.

3. MY TEENAGE YEARS

My teenage years were all about new experiences and it's difficult to choose a defining moment. Maybe it was my first kiss, because it was *sooo* good, but there was also my first heartbreak, as well as the day I went onstage and discovered my superpower. Of course, none of it would have happened the way it did if it hadn't been for my mum having another of her brilliant ideas . . .

Drama audition

I wanted to be a policewoman when I was eleven years old. So when Mum came home one day and suggested I do an audition for the Central Junior Television Workshop (CJTW), a drama club for kids, I told her I wasn't interested.

'Mum, acting isn't for me. I don't want to do it.'

My mum was insistent. Her friend Diane had a daughter called Tammy and Tammy had got into the CJTW and was really enjoying it. Twenty-five places had just come up and they were holding auditions.

'Just go along to the audition,' Mum said. 'It'll be great if you get in. You'll have stuff to do in the evenings instead of playing out every night. You'll do drama and plays and then TV shows will cast you . . .'

I suppose she just wanted to get me off the street and doing something more structured, but it sounded to me like I would be living her dream more than my own. After all, she was the one who loved show business. I wanted to be a copper.

Why is she trying to get me into this when I don't want to do it? I wondered.

'I'm telling you, you'll love it,' she said. 'Go to the audition. You may not get in but just go along and try!'

It turned out to be the best thing she could ever have suggested. I had a really good time at the audition and was amazed to find that I was quite good at the improvisational games they set up for us. I could make stuff up on the spot without a second thought.

Mum was right. This is great!

I was really enjoying myself until they brought out a script for us to read aloud. Oh, no, I thought, with a sinking heart. I'm going to be rubbish at this.

It was only three months since I'd got my glasses and I still wasn't the best of readers. I was terrified of reading aloud.

I made my excuses and took the script into the toilet, hoping there would be enough time for me to memorize it. There was a boy in there already looking over his script. 'Are you not great at reading, either?' I asked him. He shook his head. 'Shall we go through it together?' He nodded.

We ran through the script together, and when we went back to the audition, we smashed it.

A couple of weeks later, I got a letter from CJTW saying I'd got through the audition. Wa-hey! But then I read on. They were inviting me back for a second audition. I've got to do it again? I thought.

Thousands of kids applied to the CJTW every year and it was really difficult to get in, so in fact I went through two more audition stages before I was finally given a place. When I got the letter saying I'd been accepted, I felt very proud of myself and also quite glad that I didn't have to do any more auditions.

Every Tuesday evening after that – and sometimes on

Thursdays too – I'd rush home from school, get changed and go off to my CJTW drama club at the Midlands Arts Centre, the MAC, which was the creative hub of Birmingham and the coolest place in the world, in my eyes. It was just brilliant at 'the workshop', as we called it, where we learnt the inside-out of television, from how to be natural onscreen to all the behind-the-scenes technical stuff with the cameras and sound. We learnt about theatre too; we did improvisation and script creation and were always working towards putting on a production. It was a fantastic opportunity. We were such lucky kids and I think my life could have turned out very differently if I'd carried on playing tennis against people's walls.

Every now and then, directors and casting directors would come and watch us and sometimes they'd pick one or two of us to audition or do a screen test. We all encouraged each other. If somebody got a part, we'd all celebrate; if someone was successful, we were never jealous. Our leader, Colin Edwards, created a lovely, nurturing environment that was all about bigging each other up and being proud of one another's successes.

I found most of it fun and easy, but reading at first sight was still a challenge and I needed to get better at it. They would give you scripts and you'd have to read them straight off; you didn't have time to look them over first.

'Read newspapers aloud at yourself in the mirror,' suggested Colin.

I took his advice and spent hours and hours reading out newspapers in front of a mirror. The more I practised, the better I became.

It's weird, because I still have an air of doubt when it comes to reading aloud all these years later. Oh, my gosh, I'm not going to be able to read this, I think, when I'm doing *This Morning* and I see the autocue come up. Even though as an adult I know I can read.

It's mad to think that I didn't start reading properly until later in life, and I'm now on one of the biggest TV shows in the UK. I wouldn't say that presenting *This Morning* is a hard job, but you need to concentrate. There are counts going on in your ears; they're telling you which camera you're on; you've got autocue, notes, your brief, interviews, and guests to keep happy. You can't take your eye off the ball. Sometimes, when I look back at my journey and think about how far I've come, it blows me away.

Acting lessons

There was nothing stage schooly about the Central Junior Television Workshop. It wasn't about whether you looked good or spoke well: if you had an accent, they didn't try to get rid of it. They took kids who had good old-fashioned natural raw talent that they could hone and nurture. They taught us how to act – how to be natural and not overplay things or overreact – and they helped us to get work.

There were about thirty-five kids in my group and we were all from different backgrounds. Some of the kids were really poor and didn't have great lives; others lived in huge houses. Either way, we were incredibly privileged to be there, learning from our teachers and their friends in the industry.

People like Lucy Davis would come in to give us tips and advice. Lucy was a talented actress – she went on to play Dawn in *The Office* with Ricky Gervais, among other things – and she gave us a talk on how to get through an audition. I just couldn't believe how good she was at reading off the cuff. She read out a script she'd never seen before, but read it so well that it was as if she'd read it a million times. We were all very impressed by her.

Lucy's dad, the comedian Jasper Carrott, also came and

did a talk. He told us that comedy has three elements to it, and that if you can make someone laugh three times at the same joke, it's a gem. Tell it once and people laugh: great. Use the same joke again to get another laugh: even better. Make them laugh a third time at the same joke: it's a winner. I never forgot it and it's always in the back of my mind when I'm working.

I got my first speaking role on TV, aged twelve, playing Katie in *Y.E.S.*, a Central TV series set around the Youth Enquiry Service detective agency, run for teenagers by teenagers. I delivered my one line of dialogue a little bit shakily. It was quite sweet, because you could see I was really, really nervous. But of course that didn't stop my mum recording it and showing it to every single person who came to the house for ever after. I think she even showed it to the postman!

I had parts in quite a few Central TV shows: I was in *News at Twelve*, a children's show, and a couple of episodes of the long-running soap opera *Crossroads*; I was in *Searching for God*, where a group of us stayed in a convent with a load of nuns, and also did a movie, *Marjorie and the Preacherman*, with John Rhys-Davies (and my mum.)

I was thirteen when I went along to audition for a kids' TV series called *Palace Hill* – a spoof of the school drama *Grange Hill* – which had started off as a sketch on a show called *Your Mother Wouldn't Like It*. I auditioned in front of one the biggest producers in television, Sue Nott, and her team, and for some reason I decided to read my part in an American accent. Yes, I was at it again!

When I'd finished, they said, 'Would you do it in an

English accent now?' And would you believe it? They said, 'We like it best in an American accent.'

So I got the part of PC – a walking, talking personal computer, who spoke with an American accent!

When *Palace Hill* was broadcast, I became a bit of a celebrity at school. Kids kept coming up to me and saying, 'Saw you on telly last night. It was absolutely amazing.'

It was nice that people thought it was cool to see me on TV, but that wasn't why I liked being part of a production: it was the thrill of excitement that went through me when the camera started rolling. I still get that feeling when I go on air at *This Morning*. I don't take it too seriously. I'm not doing brain surgery – it's TV, it's supposed to be fun. So for me, it's like going to a party.

What's going to happen next? I think, with a nervous tremor of pleasure. It's the anticipation, the excitement. I just love it!

Life lessons

Belonging to the workshop gave me confidence and a sense that my ideas were worth listening to. Before I started there, I probably would have kept quiet in certain situations, but now, if I had an idea, I wasn't shy about putting it across, even to the adults, and if my ideas weren't taken up, I was cool with it.

I came into my own at the workshop, and over the years that followed I grew up in all kinds of ways. I gained a much better understanding of other people and how to make them feel good about themselves: how to be kind and nurturing, and how to pick them up if they were struggling. We did a lot of improvisations. If I was in a scene with someone and could see that they didn't know what to do next, I learnt to jump in and help them out, maybe even take the scene in a completely different direction.

For instance, someone might introduce a new idea and say, 'When you made that telephone call . . .'

Even if it's the first you've heard of it, you wouldn't say, 'I didn't make that telephone call!' You'd work with them and say, 'What about that telephone call?'

You have to look after each other if you want to improvise well. It's all about respecting and being kind to others.

As I was in with a great group of people, we developed a really strong bond. We loved and trusted each other, and you could see that in our work.

Most of the people I met at the workshop are still working in the industry. Some have become really famous, like Samantha Morton, who's been nominated for an Oscar, and Felicity Jones, who starred in *The Theory of Everything* with Eddie Redmayne. Some went into soaps like *Coronation Street* and *Emmerdale*, others into TV drama or music.

I never thought I was as good at acting as everybody else in our group, but what I did have was passion, enthusiasm, and I was a really good learner. I'm like a sponge and can learn things dead quick. Just show me what I've got to do and I'll get on with it. My attitude is really good. Sometimes attitude, passion and enthusiasm can outweigh knowledge, because if you haven't got those, you're not going anywhere!

As well as television work, we did a lot of live theatre training. We were taught to a professional level: we had to know our scripts, understand lighting, sound, voice projection and camera angles. We were not allowed to get it wrong.

There was never anyone on the side of the stage ready with the lines if we needed a prompt. We couldn't say, 'Give us the line.' There was none of that. You didn't even have that option. 'If you forget your line, you're going to have to find a way out of the situation and improvise,' our teachers told us. 'And everyone else has to have your back to make sure that nobody notices you've got it wrong.'

It was very disciplined and we took it so, so seriously.

Sometimes the workshop would give new writers the

chance to devise an original script with us, which would usually start with improvisations. We'd throw around some ideas and talk things through with the writers. Then they'd go away and produce a theatre piece based on the work we'd done.

Theatre was exciting because it was live and you only had one chance to get it right, although that could be overwhelming too. I'll never forget the nerves that built up as I prepared to go onstage for *Man of Substance*, one of the plays we had devised at the workshop with a new writer. We were lucky enough to stage it at the Swan Theatre in Stratford-upon-Avon, which isn't a huge venue, but seats 430 people on three sides of the stage and was going to be packed with our families and friends. I was set to be the first actor to go onstage and it was my job to captivate the whole audience with my monologue. Oh. My. God. The workshop had hired the theatre for only one night and I knew there wouldn't be a second chance to do it: I had to get it right there and then.

The night before the show, I had a dream that I was going to forget all my lines. It was the classic actor's nightmare and it really heightened my nerves the next morning. As the minutes counted down to my entrance onstage, I could feel myself getting all hot and flustered under my costume, which was a long dress with a basque top. It was the most nerve-racking experience ever.

Before long, I was shaking all over. 'Why did I agree to open the play with this monologue?' I kept asking myself.

The time came to go on. I walked onstage, and before I'd even said anything, the whole auditorium started clapping. It was ever so weird because, in that moment, I thought, I've got this! and became another person. I'm like Beyoncé and her alter ego, Sasha Fierce – as soon as I see the stage lights and the audience, I change into somebody else and there's no stopping me: I just want people to be entertained and enjoy the show.

Suddenly, I knew all my lines – and I went for it and pulled it off. That led to everyone else coming on and being amazing because we had that effect on each other. We only ever wanted each other to be good. We'd listen in backstage and will each other on; we'd log all the jokes that worked and clap silently when someone did something well.

It was a brilliant night. Everyone was happy at the end because it couldn't have gone better. That was the night I discovered that I really like being onstage. I like the feeling that nervous energy gives me. It feels like a superpower: I get a physical buzz; it's my drug. It spurs me on.

I found my confidence in performing and learnt from the challenges it presented to me: getting my acting right, overcoming nerves and having to trust in my inner self and go out onstage. I wasn't pushy or ambitious: I just enjoyed the camaraderie we shared and expressing myself through acting. One of my favourite roles was the reporter I played in *King of the City*, another original production we had devised at the workshop through improvisation. It was about a boxer with big ambitions and I was one of four reporters who wanted to get the scoop from him when he won his first big match and became famous.

Our costumes were green jackets, hats, shirts and trousers. Unfortunately, my jacket didn't fit me, because I was a big girl, so I had to use my own jacket instead. I still looked good – I had the same hat and shirt as everybody else – but I looked different because my jacket was black. How are we going to make this work? I thought.

Then it came to me. You know what? We can make anything work, I decided. And instead of it being a problem, I just said to everyone, 'If I look different, it's because I'm the leader, aren't I? I'm the chief reporter.'

In my mind, my character instantly became the boss. I wasn't really the boss – I just changed it up – and then the character started to grow. Next, the other three actors started seeing me as the boss and started to extend their characters: 'Okay, then, I'm the dippy one'; 'And I'm the funny one!' So in my bigness – in not being able to fit into one of the green jackets and having to use my own black jacket – we found purpose.

It went from 'How are we going to make this work?' to 'We can make this work even better.'

I realized then that it doesn't matter that I'm different, because I have the ability to adapt and overcome things.

Doing auditions and being rejected gave us all a strength that we took into later life. If you try to make it in acting, you're going to have to take the knockbacks. We all knew what it felt like to be turned down for a job. We had to learn how to be resilient. You don't just give up. You pick yourself up, keep going, and then you do another audition. If you get knocked back, it doesn't matter: you keep on striving.

In that sense, my time at the workshop gave me the confidence to go for anything I wanted. I never had the feeling that I couldn't do something. It was always: go for it and see what happens. I began to enjoy auditioning, so getting the job became a by-product of something I enjoyed anyway. The fun is in the journey, isn't it?

If you enjoy the graft, it becomes something you like doing, even with all the preparation and insecurity that go with it. You feel excited, even though you're thinking, Are they going to like me? Oh, I've got to learn these lines!

Getting a part is amazing, of course. But if you enjoy the process, even if you don't get it, you're still having fun.

It's a big help if you believe that where you are now is exactly where you're supposed to be, as I do. If you haven't got a job at this moment, it's all right, because it's all part of your journey. Just keep going and enjoying life. See it as one big movie that has sad moments and has amazing moments. Enjoy your movie as it's playing, and reach for that happy ending.

Times have been flipping hard, with Covid, haven't they? We've all been going through the sad part of the movie. We've had lonely times when we can't see our loved ones and we've had people dying around us. We've had our ups and downs — lots of them — and it's all part of life. But instead of stressing about it and getting down, let's look forward to our happy ending once we're through this.

That's how I live my life, waiting for my happy ending.

Friendships

At the age of thirteen, I left home and went to Nottingham for three months to film *Palace Hill*. Me and the rest of the cast stayed at the Hotel Victoria in the centre of town, which wasn't particularly smart by today's standards, but it was GREAT. The carpets had crazy diamond patterns and smelt of mothballs; the bathroom taps were reduced to a dribble in the morning and evening, when everyone was having a bath. But can you imagine how brilliant it was for a thirteen-year-old to be living in a hotel – any hotel – for three months, with a load of her mates? The feeling of freedom was out of this world.

There were two branches of the Central Junior Television Workshop, the main branch being in Nottingham, where *Palace Hill* was filmed. There were kids from both branches in the show. They were all really talented but the most talented of all, in my eyes, was Richard de Sousa, who had starred in *Y.E.S.* and *News at Twelve* and now had a leading role in *Palace Hill*. Richard was the funniest kid I'd ever met. He had a natural ability for comedy and could do improvisations that made you laugh out loud. I used to watch him, thinking, I want to be as good as he is! He was really good off the cuff.

Every kid who appeared in *Palace Hill* had to have a chaperone, by law, and Richard's mum, a little Portuguese woman, was my chaperone as well as his. My mum was happy that Mrs de Sousa was my chaperone because she knew she was quite strict. My mum wouldn't want any boys in my room. She'd want me to go to bed nice and early, and to do my schoolwork every day. She wanted her daughter to be looked after and protected. I was a virgin when I went to Nottingham and she wanted me to stay that way until I came home – and probably for the rest of my life, if she had anything to do with it! And Mrs de Sousa shared the same morals and values as my mum.

To be honest, though, Mrs de Sousa had her work cut out keeping an eye on Richard, who was always getting into trouble. She was very protective of her son. 'Richard! Richard!' you'd hear her calling. 'Where are you? What are you doing? Come here now!' It used to drive her mad when he came into my room. 'Richard, Richard, you're not allowed in Alison's room!' she'd screech.

It really made me laugh. One time he sneaked into my room to have a chat about who we fancied in the show, and while we were talking, he started tiptoeing slowly towards the door. What is he doing? I thought.

In a flash, he opened it and Mrs de Sousa fell into my room! It was pure comedy: Richard knew her so well that he'd guessed she'd be listening in on the conversation.

On our first day of filming, we were told to meet downstairs in the hotel lobby at 8.30 a.m. I was up bright and early, but as I was taking the lift downstairs, the overhead light started flickering, I was thrown into darkness and the lift lurched to a halt halfway between the first and ground floor. Oh, no! I've overloaded it! I thought. I could see the lobby down below through a narrow gap in the doors.

'Has the lift stopped working? Is someone in there?' I heard Richard asking.

'Richard!' I yelled. 'It's me! I'm stuck.'

Richard started laughing. 'I can't believe it,' he called up to me. 'Of all the people to get stuck in a lift, it had to be you.'

I had to wait an hour for someone to come along and prise the doors open so that I could climb out, which was embarrassing. But Richard found it hilarious, even though we were late for our very first day on set.

Over the next few weeks, Richard and I made friends with Ladene Hall, who was at the Nottingham branch of the workshop and also had a part in *Palace Hill*. Me, Richard and Ladene became a really tight unit. We were always together: if you saw one, you saw the others. Even when Ladene and Richard started going out with each other, I was there, because Richard was only allowed to go to Nottingham to see Ladene if I was with him. (I don't think he told his mum he had a girlfriend.) We're still the best of friends to this day.

One of the perks of working on *Palace Hill* was that we were each given a daily allowance of around twenty pounds – and not only that: they also gave us lunch on set, so we basically had twenty pounds to spend on ourselves every day. We were rich! Since me and Richard both loved Chinese food – and it was only something we ever had as a treat back home – we went for dinner at the same Chinese restaurant every night for about three months.

On the last night of filming, we told the owners, 'We've been coming here every night for three months, but you're not going to see us again. We're going back to Birmingham tomorrow.'

Hearing this, they said, 'In that case, we've got a little farewell present for you.'

Richard and I looked at each other in excitement. Amazing! We're going to get a free dinner.

We ordered our food, thinking we'd definitely be getting it free after all the money we'd spent, night after night.

Well, I'm not even joking: they came out with a shot-sized glass of diet cola and that was our present for coming to the restaurant every night. It wasn't even a half pint: it was a tiny, miniature glass of diet cola.

'Da-da! This is to say thank you!'

We couldn't believe it. 'Oh, that's so generous,' we said, trying hard not to dissolve into giggles – and we still laugh about that moment whenever we remember it.

One of the *Palace Hill* chaperones had a massive house and used to invite everyone over when any of us had a birthday. That was where I met Emma, who wasn't at the workshop but was friends with someone who was. Emma turned out to be a kindred spirit. About three minutes after we met each other, we realized we had everything in common. We didn't live too far from one another. We were both big girls. We shared a love of Chinese food, the cinema and going on the bus into town. I loved Bros and Five Star. She loved Bros and Five Star. We even liked the same type of boys. We bonded like superglue. Actually, better than superglue, because it never sticks things for very long, does it?

On a Saturday, I'd go into town on the 33 bus and head to the Rotunda, a circular skyscraper where everybody met up with their mates. It was an iconic landmark – you couldn't miss it – and it had a Coca-Cola sign at the top, back in the day. The ramp on the right of the Rotunda led down to Birmingham market, where Mum used to send me every single week with ten pounds to get the vegetables and the meat for her Saturday Soup: the chocho, pumpkin, yam, potatoes, sweet potatoes and beef. I loved the vibe when I went out and about in Birmingham. Brummie people are really friendly, not scared to have a chat with you. You could be in London and not speak to anybody all day long, because everyone's so busy that they don't look up – but in Birmingham we look up from the ground and we say hello.

People in Birmingham are kind and generous, and they look out for their communities. You'd never feel ashamed to go next door and ask for a spare egg; you know they'd do the same, so it's not a big deal. Brummies are nice, down-to-earth people – what you see is what you get. Some people don't like our accent, but the truth is, it's one of the warmest accents you'll ever come across. And for some reason, whenever I meet someone from Birmingham, my accent gets stronger and I start calling them 'Babs'!

When I met up with Emma in town, we'd usually go to the cinema, have a look around the Body Shop, try out all the perfumes in Rackhams – literally spray ourselves down with every single perfume going – and experiment with different bits of makeup. Then we'd head to McDonald's, buy a meal with a toy for 99 pence and go home on the bus eating chips. We always sat on the top deck of the bus where everybody smoked: we didn't care if we ended up stinking of cigarettes, because it was the cool place to sit.

Nothing can replace the friendships you have with old mates and, to this day, Emma is a true friend, one of those people who is always there for you. She's so kind and has a lovely generous spirit. When she lost her mum to cancer about eleven years ago, I went through it with her, every step of the way; and when my mum died of cancer in 2020, she was there for me when I turned to her for support.

Emma knew my mum for almost all her life and they got on really well, so I found it funny that my mum never said to Emma, 'Call me Maria.'

I understand that Mum was big on etiquette, like Auntie Mavis, and that when we were growing up we all addressed our friends' parents as 'Mr' or 'Mrs'. Still, you would have thought that when Emma became an adult, my mum would have asked her to start calling her Maria. But no, it was always 'Mrs Foster'. And Emma accepted that.

For years Emma and I have shared a problem in that we both struggle to lose weight. It's Emma I phone when I want to talk about my weight issues and vice versa, because we both get it. I know Emma's deepest secrets and she knows mine – and we're not telling! We've been confiding in each other for more than thirty years now – I hope we'll still be ringing each other in thirty years' time to say, 'You'll never guess what! Don't tell anyone, but I . . .'

'Oh, no! You didn't!'

First kiss

When I was fourteen, I had my first kiss at the Midlands Arts Centre in Birmingham with a guy called Caleb, who went on to star in *Blood Brothers* in the West End and is now an ambulance driver. It was the best kiss I've ever had – I've never had a better kiss in my life, honestly.

That kiss happened in none other than the dressing-room toilet, which wasn't the most romantic of places, but it felt absolutely amazing at the time. I was on cloud nine when I came out of the toilet. I don't think I ever spoke to Caleb again, though. Not while we were at workshop, anyway. So that was the end of the story. We had a kiss and then didn't speak again for about ten years!

I'm back in touch with Caleb now and spoke to him recently. 'Are you okay with me talking about how I kissed you?' I asked.

'Yeah, don't worry about it,' he said.

His wife was in the background and said, 'Yes, fine!'

'You didn't speak to me afterwards,' I told him.

'Yes, I did!' he protested.

'You didn't.'

'Well, I remember the kiss but I can't remember what happened afterwards,' he admitted.

'You remember the kiss?'

He paused. 'I can't remember *exactly* what it was like, because by the time I kissed you, I'd already kissed about six girls.'

'Oh, my God, I feel so used!' I shrieked.

It was an amazing kiss for me, but not so memorable for him, obviously, lol.

Rebel days

When I look back it feels as if we were constantly having fun at the workshop: we were loud, we were messy, we'd play Truth or Dare, and Spin the Bottle in the dressing rooms; we did sponsored silences and sponsored sleepovers at people's houses. We were normal teenagers being teenagers, growing up and having a laugh. It was all about the lols.

Ladene and I often used to stay at each other's houses and I went through a phase of thinking she was the coolest person in the world. I just love her and everything about her *so much*, I thought.

Teenage girls feel everything so intensely, don't they? I mean, I absolutely loved Ladene. I still do.

One morning, when Ladene was staying with me, we left my house to go to my local launderette to dry some clothes we'd washed. We couldn't hang them up and leave them to dry naturally, we had to wear them ASAP! The launderette was at the top of a really steep hill so we asked my mum to drop us there on her way to work.

On our way back down the hill, about half an hour later, Ladene pulled out a cigarette. She was a smoker at the time; it was cool, back then. I didn't drink and I definitely didn't smoke, as I knew my mum would kill me if she ever caught me smoking. But Ladene was a rebel.

She lit her cigarette and started smoking it. 'Go on, have a drag,' she said, offering it to me.

'No, I don't smoke. I'm not into it.'

'Just try it,' she said. 'See if you like it.'

I had a reluctant drag of this cigarette. 'No, man, I don't like it.' I shook my head in disgust.

'Have another go,' she said.

I had another drag and, as I was trying to inhale the smoke, I heard someone behind me screaming, 'Alison! Alison!'

I turned round to see my mum at the top of the hill shouting at the top of her voice, 'Alison, get here now!'

I froze. 'Oh, no, my mum's seen us smoking!' I whimpered. 'What's she doing there? I thought she'd gone to work.'

If my mum caught me smoking, it meant one thing and one thing only: the death penalty. I'm going to die, I thought. My world was going to end, because I never wanted to disappoint my mum. I only wanted to make her proud.

I started having a panic attack; and Ladene was panicking and thinking, Oh, no, Alison's mum is going to think I'm a bad influence!

(Which she was.)

I crushed the cigarette in my hand and felt no pain whatsoever. I chucked it on the ground. Then I reached into my pocket to pull out some chewing gum, to hide the smell of smoke on my breath.

I stuffed some gum into my mouth and frantically

started chewing it. 'Here, have some of this!' I told Ladene. 'You can't smell of cigarettes when you're talking to my mum.'

I'm chomping gum. I'm panicking. My heart is racing at nineteen to the dozen. We're running back up this hill. We're out of breath. The palm of my hand is throbbing.

'Look how angry my mum is!' I kept saying to Ladene. 'We're going to die! This is your fault. You made me smoke that cigarette.'

'I'm sure it'll be fine. It'll be fine!' she gasped, trying to reassure me.

'You won't ever be allowed to come to my house again!' I yelled at her. 'She will not allow you to come back now she's seen you smoking!'

We got to the top of the hill and I was panting and crying because I knew I was going to get into so much trouble.

'Alison!' my mum called.

'Yes, Mummy,' I sobbed, about to fall to my knees and kiss her feet.

'Alison, did you see what happened?'

I stopped. 'No, what happened?'

She pointed to her car, which was parked crookedly by the side of the road. It had a dented front bumper and a smashed headlight. 'I've just crashed my car! Up here, on the hill, after dropping you off.'

My tears turned to happiness. 'Oh, no, Mum! How did it happen? Are you okay?'

It was a horrible situation because I was relieved and happy that she'd crashed her car rather than seen me smoking.

Ladene found it hilarious and couldn't stop laughing. We'd built this whole scenario about how she'd never be able to come to my house again, all for nothing.

All the same, I never smoked another cigarette.

Teenage days

I was into boys as a teenager, but as a girl with a fuller figure I knew boys weren't into girls who looked like me. I wasn't bothered, because I was mainly into having fun and making people laugh. I'm not the sort of person someone's going to fall in love with straight away: I'm more of a slow burn, and it's my personality that people fall in love with. I can literally see the change in their eyes when it happens.

The best-looking guy at the workshop was Neil Newbon, the son of the sports commentator Gary Newbon. I was completely in love with Neil, from a distance. I remember going to his house and getting tongue-tied when I met his dad. But my next proper crush – after Caleb and my first kiss – was Hugo, who was also at the workshop. Hugo was one of the funniest people I knew. We had a great time together and were really good friends. I really fancied him in my teenage years. Nothing happened between us, but it was obvious that I really liked him and everyone knew I was into him. I'd probably even told him as much. I'm sure he knew, anyway.

When the workshop finished on a Tuesday or a Thursday, some of us often hung around for a bit and chilled out before we went home. Me and Hugo used to go for long walks along the canal and I hoped my personality was slowly luring him in. It certainly felt as if we had a strong connection. We said things to each other like, 'If we ever lose touch, let's meet in this exact location in exactly ten years' time.'

When the Nottingham branch of the workshop announced they were putting on a disco, it was big news. We went by coach and you could feel the excitement rising. The moment we got off, I rushed to find Ladene and get on the dance floor.

It was a really great night. Ladene and I never stopped dancing. Then, about halfway through the evening, I looked across the room and saw Hugo kissing a girl from the Nottingham group.

I was mortified. It was such a shock. I stopped dancing and ran to the toilets, closely followed by Ladene. 'What is it? What's wrong?' she asked me.

I burst into tears. 'Did you see . . . Hugo . . . kissing . . . that girl?'

I was crying so hard that my chest was heaving. If Hugo was going to kiss anyone at the disco, it should have been ME. It was the first time I'd cried over a boy and I felt so hurt and betrayed.

On the way back on the coach, I gave Hugo the cold shoulder when he tried to talk to me.

'What's the matter?' he kept asking.

'Nothing. Just don't speak to me,' I said, staring stonily out of the window.

I couldn't even look at him. I was absolutely devastated.

Our friendship survived, though. I'm not one to bear

grudges, and me and Hugo had a really strong connection. We still do, in fact: we can say anything to each other. And he was funny — and I find you can't be upset for too long with someone who makes you laugh, because it's such a nice feeling.

New York

In 1991, when I'd just turned sixteen, I went on a CJTW acting student exchange trip to New York. Central Television put money towards it, but most of the cost had to come from our parents – and as Mum really wanted me to go, she worked her socks off to pay for the flights. Bless her!

Imagine, a group of teenage kids going to New York without their parents! For two weeks during the Easter holidays! It was just amazing, even though we stayed in a slightly dodgy hotel on the East Side for the first week. I had a shock when we were being shown to our rooms, because the walls of the lobby and staircase were covered with weird, semi-pornographic murals. What is this place? I thought, feeling slightly worried. I didn't think my mum would be happy if she saw those pictures.

We were in New York to create a piece of theatre with some kids from a downtown performing arts school. It was in quite a dangerous area and we were searched for guns and knives at the entrance every day, which was intimidating but felt kind of cool to us kids, although obviously it wasn't cool at all. We spent the mornings creating an improvisational piece of theatre and went off sightseeing in the afternoons.

The second week, we left the hotel, split into twos and threes, and went to stay at the students' houses with their families. Me and another girl stayed at a guy called Hector's house and his parents really looked after us. It was brilliant seeing how New York kids lived their life, what their schools were like and how they dealt with stuff. It was definitely up there with visiting the Empire State Building and going on the Circle Cruise. Obviously, being sixteen and away from home, I fell in love with Hector, our host. But he was interested in the other girl, so I got blown out. Gutted.

Back in Birmingham I went straight into my GCSE term and did really well in my exams: I passed them all and even got a B in biology, which I was really chuffed about. I can't tell you how much graft went into those GCSEs. I did well because I wanted to. There was no way I was going to fail.

I was asked to compère a students' end-of-year show. It sounded like a walk in the park – all I had to do was introduce a series of sketches and songs in front of an audience of parents and teachers. In reality, though, it wasn't as easy as it sounded because when somebody wasn't ready to come on, I'd be told, 'Just go out there and speak for five minutes, will you?'

I kept having to go out there and have a little laugh with the audience while we waited for the next act to come on. It was like doing stand-up – without a script or any rehearsal.

'You had everyone laughing and kept the flow going,' my sister said, at the end. 'You should definitely do that for a living!'

By then I'd decided that I wanted acting to be my career, so I applied to drama school and got into ALRA, the Academy of Live and Recorded Arts.

'We will be modifying your accent as part of your training,' they said.

'All right, then,' I replied, even though I wasn't sure what they meant by that.

When I realized that they wanted me to get rid of my Birmingham accent, I started to have doubts. You know what? I'm happy the way I am, I thought. I love who I am. This is my voice. Deal with it.

In the end, I didn't have the funds to pay my own way through ALRA and didn't secure a sponsorship grant, so I didn't go. Perhaps that was a good thing, because if I had, I might be speaking like Princess Anne now. I don't think I looked very hard for the sponsorship, to be honest. Instead I went to a local college and did an A level in performing arts, which I passed with a nice B grade.

I found it hard to let go of the workshop when I reached eighteen and it was time to leave. I volunteered to help the leader audition all the new people, but there came a point when I knew I couldn't hang on for ever. I had my own car and was driving around. I had grown up. It was time to go out into the world and make my own life.

Just before I was eighteen, I decided to go on this mad diet. I wanted to be smaller and managed to go from seventeen stone down to thirteen and a half. I was chuffed that I'd done so well: I felt happier about how I looked and started wearing ripped jeans and cool clothes.

Suddenly, Hugo started taking a bit of an interest in me.

Bearing in mind that he hadn't chosen to kiss me at the disco a few years before, I thought, This is weird. How fickle are you?

We went to play tennis one day and had a really good game. 'Do you want to come back to my place?' he asked afterwards.

'Yeah, all right, then.'

Our friend Chung was with us. We were up in Hugo's room, and when Chung went to get a drink from downstairs, Hugo kissed me and we started getting off with each other. Oh, my God, I can't believe this! I thought. I was still totally in love with Hugo.

But when Chung came back I started to have doubts. 'I don't want to go any further with you, because you've just proved how fickle you are,' I told Hugo.

'What are you on about?' he asked, looking puzzled.

'You didn't want me when I was fifteen and now you want a piece just because I've lost a little bit of weight!' I said.

'Not at all,' he protested. 'I really like you.'

I wasn't having it. 'Absolutely a million per cent the only reason you're interested in me is because I've lost weight.'

Maybe it was my own demons telling me this, but I felt really upset about it. And that was that. For then, at least – because there's a postscript to this story, as it happens . . .

Can you guess who I lost my virginity to at the age of twenty-one? I know, I was so old! What was I waiting for?

Well, I was waiting for that big romantic moment, but then I found out that Hugo had slept with one of my friends and I was so jealous that I decided to lose my virginity to him. Looking back, it had to be Hugo – and I'm glad it was him, because he was such a good friend that it wasn't awkward in any way. In fact, it was great! Once we'd got the initial 'operation' out of the way, I wanted to try every position going. I was twenty-one – I was a woman in my prime – and I was ready for this, man. I'd waited so long that I thought, I don't know when the next session is going to be, so if I'm going to try this, I'm going to do it to the fullest!

He was rather tired when I left him. I definitely wore him out.

I spoke to him the other day and he said, 'Make sure you tell everyone it was really big!' lol.

'Okay,' I said. 'This is going to be an honest, authentic book, Hugo, but if you want me to lie, I will.'

All the men I've been with go on to become really good friends. They don't want to let the Hammond go, babes. Once you have a taste, that's it, you're hooked.

Apart from Caleb, obviously, who can't even remember the best kiss I ever had in my life.

4. FINDING MY WAY

The real world

It took me a while to find my niche in life. I had dreams of becoming a professional actor when I left college in 1993, but struggled to get the parts. I did some work on *Doctors*, but after that my acting career fizzled out and I realized it was time to get a normal job and start paying my way in the world, like my mate Emma. As a hairdresser earning quite good money, Emma was always paying for me to go to the cinema, or have a Chinese. I wanted to be generous back. And pay my bills too.

I'd been working Saturdays at Shared Earth, a lovely shop in Birmingham that sold ethically sourced goods from around the world: beautiful Malawian pottery, gorgeous Moroccan jewellery and clothes. After I left college, I took on more shifts there because the owner very kindly gave me time off if I had an audition for TV or theatre, and when she had the idea to make a video to promote the shop, she asked me to present it. She hired a video production team in York and I went up there to film it. 'You've done a wonderful job, Alison!' she said, when she saw the final cut.

To my surprise, I found I was actually quite good at presenting. I guess that was where it all started! Having said that, although *This Morning* was a staple in our house growing up, back then when I was watching Richard and Judy I never imagined that I would – or could – ever be one of the hosts. Even if I thought I'd probably be rather good at it, given the chance, you didn't see people who looked like me presenting daytime television.

Next, I worked at Jeffrey Rogers, a clothes shop, and in the evenings I was the coat-check girl in the cloakroom of Bakers nightclub in the centre of town. People would give me a pound as a deposit for their ticket and I'd hang their coat up; they'd go into the club and have a really good time while I chilled out in the cloakroom. Then when they came back, gave me their tickets and got their coats, they'd be a bit drunk and say, 'Keep the pound!' By the end of the night, I'd sometimes have seventy or eighty pounds – occasionally, I came away with a hundred quid! – so I was quite sad when that job ended.

I signed on with a temping agency that sent me off to work for companies like Transco and Cable & Wireless and I still don't understand what I did for Transco. It was something to do with shipper codes, but I can't tell you what a shipper code is. I haven't got a clue. Still, I managed to work with shipper codes on and off for about three years.

It was no different when I went to Cable & Wireless. I couldn't tell you what the job was, really. All I knew was I was getting paid to do it. I remember going in there just before Christmas, when they needed loads of extra people. 'If you manage to do a thousand socket points by Christmas, you'll get a bonus of five hundred pounds,' they told us, at the start of the job.

I didn't ask myself what socket points were or what I was doing with them. I just thought, Five hundred quid? I'm not missing out on this.

I quickly worked out that some of the socket-point applications were a lot bigger than others, and that the small ones took a lot less time to complete. So every morning I used to go through the pack and get all the small applications, which was a bit naughty of me but I was desperate to make my target. Lo and behold, I smashed it and got that five hundred quid.

And then I got taxed on it! Gutted.

After working with that level of tedium, you can imagine how I felt when a Theatre In Education company approached me about working with them. Yes, thrilled. Theatre In Education (TIE) uses drama and interactive theatre to raise awareness among kids of school age about a range of issues. So I'd be devising and acting out scenarios about anything from stranger danger to the implications of smoking, doing drugs and teenage pregnancy. Bring it on!

I was so glad to be back doing what I loved best and worked with a few different companies – Gazebo, Women In Theatre and Catalyst Theatre. We used to create a play around a certain issue, work out a teacher's pack, then go out and look for sponsorship. At one point, I was in a play about road safety with Catalyst Theatre that Toyota sponsored. Toyota gave us a van, which was branded for Catalyst Theatre, and we went on the road, staying in B-and-Bs along the way.

It was hard work, because we did absolutely everything.

We'd go into a school in the morning and set up the stage, put on a play, do the workshop and take it all down again. Then we'd drive to the next school to do it in the afternoon, and the same the next day and the next. It was tiring but it felt good going into communities and helping kids to make the right decisions in their lives, and I really loved the acting and improvisational side of it. So whenever I got that call from a TIE company, saying, 'Alison, we've got two months' work here. Do you want to take it on?' I dropped everything.

I juggled a lot of different jobs in my twenties. I'd maybe do two or three months of Theatre In Education, then six months Cable & Wireless, YAWN, two months Theatre In Education, a bit of time at Transco, YAWN, work in a shop and do a few shifts at my local cinema. That's how I used to roll. I was fluid and went with what was happening. Nothing was ever really the same.

Obviously my core was acting and it was what I wanted to do, so Theatre In Education would always come first. I was happiest when I was entertaining people and expressing myself through drama. Wherever I was, I always tried to bring fun and drama to the floor, though. We'd be sitting around the desk doing shipper codes on our computers at Transco, and when lunchtime came and we started eating our food, I'd say to my group, 'I know, let's do a bit of a tune! Jo, I want you to go "sh-sh-sh" and, Samesh, you go "ba-ba, ba-ba-ba!"' Meanwhile I'd hum, someone else would drum a rhythm with their pen and we'd make our own little orchestra with our mouths and the bits and pieces we had at our desks.

It made everyone laugh so much. People still phone me up and say, 'I miss our time at Transco.'

Which is really saying something, believe me, because doing shipper codes can be flipping tedious (especially if you don't know what they are).

Making the most

I hated being out of work, so I was willing to do almost anything that paid the bills. I was often asked, 'Can you type?'

Straight answer: no, I couldn't type a bean. But my approach to all kinds of work was usually to say, 'Yes, I can do it,' and deal with it later.

That was how I got the job of typist at an important department of social services, where they looked after children's welfare. 'Are you an actual touch typist?' they asked me, on my first day there.

Since I could only type with one finger and sometimes got it stuck in the typewriter, I felt I couldn't lie outright. 'I'll be honest with you,' I said, 'I'm not really a typist, but I will be able to do the job all the same.'

For some reason, this answer satisfied them.

The other typists and I had to type out reports handwritten by the department's social workers, which meant having to decipher their often illegible handwriting. Some of the reports were about children being abused and they were so heartbreaking that I learnt to turn my mind off as I typed them, because if I focused on what I was reading, it would just make me cry.

I was the slowest typist by far and was always expecting

to be sacked. I probably managed to type two reports a day while everyone else was doing ten. But I never got into trouble because they liked having me around. Amid the trauma of typing and filing these emotionally devastating reports, we used to have a lot of fun. I entertained the team with my dance moves, cartwheels across the room and handstands up the wall. I'd go across the road to McDonald's, bring bags of food back to the office that we'd all eat together. We got on so well that we went to the cinema after work, or out to eat.

It was a really sad department and I was bringing the joy, the laughter and the lols.

'When you come in, it's like a breath of fresh air,' they used to say. 'When you're not here, we're all depressed and it doesn't feel right.'

'Even though I'm really bad at typing?'

'We don't care. Just come in.'

My banter was so uplifting that the other typists were happy to cover my back and do my work for me. Honestly, they were so good to me.

One of the social workers would ask me, 'Have you finished that report yet?'

'Nearly there,' I'd assure her. Then I'd sidle over to Sharon or one of the other typists. 'Babe,' I'd say, 'I've got Linda on my back. Can you do this report for me?'

'Yeah, go on, here you go.'

Every single typist there, apart from me, was a proper QWERTY-trained typist. I used to look on in amazement as their fingers flew across the keyboard. 'How do you do that?' I'd ask.

Fifteen minutes later, I'd go back to the social worker with the finished report. 'Well done, Alison, that's lovely!' she'd say, as she looked it over.

Typing all day long meant I did actually get quite good at it. I'm quick now. I started off using one finger, then two fingers – and ended up using six. I was still too slow for the job and probably shouldn't have been there, but I wasn't idle: I was up for working hard and always offering to do any job other than typing. Sometimes they'd let me spend the day filing instead. Phew!

I really enjoyed that job and was gutted when it came to an end and I started working as an usherette in a cinema. Little did I know what adventures life had in store for me.

'Fancy going on holiday somewhere?' Emma asked me, one day. 'I'm thinking Tunisia. I saw a really good deal in the travel agent's window yesterday and thought I'd ring up.'

'Tunisia?' I said. 'I'm in. Is the food any good?'

Holida-ay

When Emma and I flew to Tunisia for two weeks with Airtours in the late 1990s, we went in search of sun, sand, sea,
R and R and maybe a little bit of a holiday romance. We
were definitely up for the lols. And we were in for a nice
surprise on that holiday, because the Tunisian men look like
models and, even better, they love a curvier woman. Result!

The Hotel Saphir was a large, airy hotel situated right on
the beach, with loads of fantastic facilities and a gorgeous
pool area. Emma and I gasped in wonder as we stepped
into the enormous marble foyer on our first day. Ooh,
Heaven really is a place on earth! After rainy Birmingham,
it felt like a palace of eternal summer. Or that was my first
impression, at least. The quality of package holidays had
definitely gone up a notch since my trips to Malta with my
mum when I was eight.

While we were waiting to check in at the reception desk,
we got talking to the hotel entertainment manager, who told
us there was a whole programme of events planned for the
fortnight ahead. 'The hotel is renowned for its nightlife and
entertainers,' he said, beaming with pride. 'Six nights a week,
there's a kids' mini disco at seven o'clock, followed by a quiz
and bingo, and then a big show or a cabaret.'

Yay! We went to the entertainment every night. We did not miss one show.

We spent our days relaxing by the pool or at the beach and wandering around town, checking out the medina and souks. Everything about Tunisia charmed us: the weather, the people, the markets and the food. Especially the food. Couscous! Shakshuka! Brik! Lablabi! Tunisia has the best food in the world – oh, my God! – and the sweets and puddings are heavenly.

One day, while we were relaxing by the huge pool, sipping a mint tea and staring happily at the blue sky above us, we got chatting to one of the entertainment crew, who seemed a bit down.

'I wish I was back in the UK,' she sighed. 'I've only just got here but I miss my boyfriend so, so much. I just want to go home. I'm hating it!' Tears started running down her cheeks.

'Oh, no, you poor thing!' we said.

'I can't bloody stand it,' she sobbed. 'And, Christ, I've got to do the mini disco tonight! How can I do the bleeding mini disco in this state?'

She looked so miserable that I said, 'Do you want me to do it for you? I've done a lot of acting and performing, so it wouldn't be a problem.'

She wiped her eyes and turned to me, blinking hard. 'Would you?'

'Yeah, I'll take over for you tonight.'

She instantly cheered up. 'Well, if you don't mind, that would be amazing. It's not a hard job but I'm no good for anything at the moment. I'm just really missing my boyfriend.'

She asked her manager if it would be okay for me to go onstage and do the mini disco in her place. He said it was fine! Health and safety . . . bothered!

So, that night, I put on a nice kid-friendly outfit, the sort of outfit I could do a bit of dancing in – my tracksuit – and went up on the rickety old hotel stage to get that mini disco popping. I played kids' songs, sang along, told jokes, made up dances on the spot and got everyone up onstage. We did a whole routine to 'I am the music man; I come from down your way and I can play . . .' We did 'Superman'; I even got some of the adults up to sing, 'Gimme hope Jo'anna'.

Everyone had a great old time and I was absolutely loving it.

Afterwards, the manager came up to me smiling from ear to ear. 'You should so do entertaining! You were made for it,' he said, vigorously shaking my hand.

'It's funny,' I said, 'because I used to be an actress, but I work in a cinema at the moment.'

He shook his head. 'You're wasted in a cinema. You really should go into entertaining abroad,' he said. I took it with a pinch of salt, but he added, 'If you want to come and join in again while you're here, you're welcome.'

The entertainer I stood in for was missing her boyfriend so much that she decided to leave. A couple of days later, the manager came up to me before dinner and said, 'Would you like to interview for the role of entertainer here at the hotel?'

'What? You want me to come for an interview while I'm on holiday?' I said.

'Yes. We can interview you here in Tunisia, and if you get the job, we'll give you a week at home to sort your life out and fly you back here to start work.'

I went to the interview. I got the job. Who would have thought that a package trip to Tunisia could change my life so dramatically?

I flew back home after the holiday ended. 'I'm only staying a week, Mum.' I said. 'I've got a job in Tunisia.'

'Really?' She was used to me doing all sorts of jobs but this was a step beyond.

'Yeah, I'm going to be an entertainments rep in a hotel.'

'Oh, my gosh! Well, it'll make a change.'

She was right about that. And you know what? I really, really needed a change.

Paradise again

Exactly a week after Emma and I got home from our holiday, I flew back out to Tunisia and became an entertainer at the Hotel Saphir. It was a full-on job: I played bowls and water polo with the guests in the pool in the morning; then in the evening I did the bingo, the quiz and a show. I also helped to sell day trips and excursions to the hotel guests. I never stopped.

Sometimes I had to do airport duties and I was in my element going to meet the holidaymakers and bringing them back on the coach. 'Welcome to Tunisia,' I used to say, once we were on our way. 'Now, the currency here is dinars. You get two dinars to your pound. Please don't drink the water from the tap. Make sure you use bottled water. However, if you're just brushing your teeth and not swallowing it, you will be okay.

'In Tunisia, it's great to know a few phrases, so "hello" is *asslema*. After three, everyone, give me a hello! One, two, three: *asslema!*

'And "goodbye" is *bisslema*. Ready? *Bisslema!*'

'So, just remember, A and B, *asslema* and *bisslema*. "Thank you" is *chokran* and "please" is *minfadlik*. There you go – some phrases for you. Now you can sit back, because I'm not going to carry on talking. Just make sure your armrests are down. No smoking on this journey, and I'll be back with you when we're near Hammamet. Enjoy your ride.'

I absolutely loved doing airport duties. It made me feel really important. These people had just arrived in a country they'd never been to before, and a lot of what they saw out of the coach window was unfamiliar and might have been a bit daunting. There were a lot of police officers on the corners of the roads, and I had to explain that they were only making sure people had all their ID papers. A lot of the houses looked unfinished, but that was because the Tunisians have a different approach to constructing their homes and build upwards, as and when a new branch of the family joins the household. I was there to keep people calm on the journey from the airport and help them check in when we got to the hotel. I loved it: I'd take the mic and say, 'Tomorrow we've got a welcome meeting at ten o'clock. Make sure you come, because our reps are going to be telling you about some great excursions . . .'

One of the top reps was a girl called Sarah. She was really, really good at selling all the great excursions to the holidaymakers. Yet from the word go I had the sense that she didn't like me. My intuition told me she wasn't happy that I had suddenly gone from being a hotel guest to working alongside her. I could feel her looking daggers at me, as if to say, 'Who is this girl? What is she doing here?'

What have I done to deserve this? I wondered. I just couldn't understand it.

The final straw came when I noticed her giving me dirty looks from her sun lounger while I was playing water polo with a group of holidaymakers in the pool. We were having a right laugh, splashing around and chasing the ball, but Sarah was scowling at us. What's her problem? I thought.

I got out of the pool and walked over to her. 'All right, babe?'

'Yes, fine,' she said.

'Oh, wicked,' I said.

I noticed that her nails had no polish on. 'I've got a nail kit in my room. Would you like me to do your nails for you?'

She looked up and smiled. 'Yes, all right then.'

I fetched my nail kit and buffed and filed her nails, and I could just tell as I did it that I was breaking through her hard exterior. She didn't like me at first but then I gave her a bit of Hammond love and literally broke down the barriers. She's been my friend ever since – and on reflection, after knowing her for twenty years, I now realize that what I thought was a scowl is just her natural resting bitch face, lol.

Sarah and I have lots of shared interests: she's also a single woman and she's a plump girl. It's the same as with my mate Emma: we have a connection over our bigness. I'm godmother to Sarah's twin boys. I even went to Canada for the christening because their dad is from Canada. And whenever I see her, we have a proper laugh reminiscing about what we got up to in Tunisia.

At one point we went out with two DJs, one each. Sarah's DJ boyfriend was Saba; he was very good-looking, with long, wavy hair. My DJ boyfriend was Ramsey; he was gorgeous and looked like a model, but was only five foot two. He reminded me a bit of Ricky Martin, actually, only shorter.

Saba and Ramsey were the worst DJs you've ever heard. They were absolutely terrible. Their idea of mixing music was to do a couple of scrapes and change the record. But because they weren't any good at it, there would be this agonizing moment of silence until the next record came on. Still, Sarah and I fell in love with them and started going out on dates with them. Since we all worked in the evenings, they'd take us to the beach for the day and sometimes we went out on boat trips.

'Let's tie a rope on the back of the boat,' Saba suggested, one sparklingly sunny afternoon. 'Everyone can hold onto it while we pull you along.'

It seemed like a good idea so he and Ramsey tied a rope on the back of this boat. There were a few of us onboard and we all got into the water, grabbed hold of the rope and someone signalled the driver to pick up speed.

Saba and Ramsey hung off the side, filming us on this old video camera they had. I won't lie, the video is funny, despite what happened. You can see everyone having a really good time, laughing and shrieking as the boat pulls them through the water on this rope. Then, as the camera moves along the line of smiling faces, it finally gets to me, right at the end of the rope, being dragged under the water, like a half-dead fish. My head isn't even visible most of the time. I'm practically drowning. It reaches a point where I have to let go of the rope but, of course, no one notices that I've let go until I'm a mile out to sea. When they finally realize and turn around and come and pick me up, the video captures everyone laughing their heads off. Finally, I get out of the water and back onto the boat, dripping like a drowned rat. It's like an extended clip from *You've Been Framed*.

Saba and Ramsey used to finish their DJ set at about three o'clock in the morning, so me and Sarah would go to bed at ten, get up at three, get dressed, put our makeup on and meet them after they'd packed up for the night. That was how much we liked them.

'Let's go for something to eat,' someone would say.

It would be four or five in the morning: we'd go to a restaurant and they'd order sheep's head. 'Have some! The cheeks are lovely,' they'd say.

We weren't tempted. 'No, it's all right. We don't want to eat sheep's head.'

'Go on, just try it.'

'Listen. We are not eating sheep's head.'

Imagine eating a sheep's head and offering us a bit of cheek and a bit of brains and saying it was lovely! Our boyfriends were absolute mingers.

'Can we just have some chicken nuggets and chips, please?'

So we'd be eating our chicken nuggets and chips while they were digging into their sheep's head, happy as Larry, sucking the bones and everything. And because we were absolutely in love with them, we didn't care.

Of course there was always drama with our boyfriends. Someone would end up being cheated on and then it was all over. The resort was one big romantic merry-go-round and people got together and split up every five minutes. We started calling it *TunEnders*. Something was always happening. It was a right giggle.

Every month, all the reps in the resort gathered to put on a variety show at a big casino near the hotel. It was the one night in the month that we'd get to see everybody else in the resort and have some fun. We'd do songs. We'd do dances. We'd do comedy. We rehearsed on the day and worked our socks off to make it a really good show.

Sometimes I hosted it, but either way I usually sang 'Mustang Sally' at some point. I was in my element and always did a Victoria Wood sketch that went down really well. It's a classic: she's in a leotard doing a bit of exercise and it really made people laugh. The Spice Girls were big then, and in another sketch Sarah would be Baby Spice and I'd be Mel B, and we did a really silly piece where we sang 'My Heart Will Go On' from *Titanic* while my friend Jason paddled around in the background, singing along in his swimming trunks. We also hired entertainers and you'd have these amazing drag queens coming on and doing comedy.

I always wanted to get the audience involved. We played lots of games and some nights we'd do men versus women quizzes. Other nights we did a donkey derby, where we raced donkeys and people would bet on them. They weren't real donkeys, by the way. They were just cards with pictures of donkeys on them. But everyone was happy with that. We'd roll a dice and move the donkeys along according to their score. You'd bet whether the red donkey, the blue donkey or the yellow donkey would win – it was all down to chance – and if you guessed correctly, you'd win some money. People loved it. A bit of gambling. It was a good night. The bingo was great too, and the quizzes. You name it, we used to do it, just to keep the clientele happy.

Just last week someone stopped me in the street and said, 'I was in Tunisia at the Hotel Saphir when you were one of the entertainers. Those nights were amazing!'

A lot of drinking went on at the resort, but I was never a big drinker because alcohol has the opposite effect on me than it does on other people. When I drink, I become a different person: I turn quiet. Alcohol makes me feel really tired, like I'm jet-lagged, and I want to go to bed. It's like my kryptonite. I've got nothing to say and nine times out of ten I'll just fall asleep.

'You are so dry when you drink,' Sarah used to say.

The one night I did have a couple of glasses of wine. I fell asleep out and about and nobody could move me. I was in a bar and I just fell asleep. It was so embarrassing. Sarah had to stay with me all night, until morning.

'What the heck?' I said, when I woke up and looked around me. Daylight was streaming in through the window of the bar. 'What are we doing here?'

'Babes, you wouldn't wake up,' Sarah said, 'so we got stuck here.'

'You are joking? They let us stay? Babes, you should have woken me up.'

'Believe me, I tried.'

'Could you not have lifted me up?'

'Er, no.'

Sarah laid down the law after that: 'Whatever you do, do not give Alison any alcohol! She can't handle it. It makes her depressed and she becomes really boring.'

To this day, my friends and family know not to give me alcohol. I do like a mojito, but although it makes me feel nice, it also makes me feel tired. Maybe at Christmas I'll have a Baileys, but I'll have it towards bedtime because I know I'm just going to want to fall asleep. Well, alcohol is a depressant, isn't it? I'm definitely not the life and soul of the party when I drink.

For me, I'd choose a lovely meal over a drink, without a doubt. You get some people, like your Sarahs and your Emmas, who would probably choose a drink over a lovely meal. Actually, maybe not Emma: Emma would probably choose the meal over a nice drink. But I'm just not that person who will choose a drink over a meal. I'd rather the food.

People ask, 'So what do you do when you're stressed?'

The answer is that I eat sweets. I love spearmint chews and other old-fashioned sweets that are full of sugar, although I try not to eat too many of them. Oh dear, but the other day I went online to order a small bag of spearmint chews and bought a three-kilo bag by mistake. Do you know how big a three-kilo bag of spearmint chews looks? There are absolutely loads of them and I'm going to have to chuck most of them away. Problem is, I can't chuck them away because I love them! Perhaps I'll just eat this lot and give them up afterwards . . .

Even more paradise

I kept going back to Tunisia to do the summer season. I loved it so much that I even decided to do the season over Christmas one year. That stint didn't go so well, unfortunately. I thought I'd be all right, but when the camel came trotting down the beach with Santa on its back, it just wasn't doing it for me, and I burst into tears.

This isn't right. I'm in this boiling-hot country when it should be cold and snowy. Santa's on a camel and doesn't even look like Santa, I thought. What am I doing here?

It was my first Christmas away from home without my mum and I was in tears all day on Christmas Day. I couldn't stop crying down the phone to her. 'I'll never do this again, Mum!' I sobbed. 'I miss you so much! I just want to be at home with you.'

'Don't worry,' she kept saying. 'You'll know for next time: don't ever go away for Christmas again.'

I think I had couscous for dinner. It wasn't right at all. I was missing my roast turkey.

The following summer, when I was twenty-five, I decided I wanted a change and went to do the season in Menorca. But I didn't really like Menorca. After one season, I told my boss, 'I'm just not feeling it here.'

I was so unhappy. I really was. I just didn't get the vibe. It was nothing like Tunisia, where I felt so at home. I think it was partly because I didn't speak the language. I'd studied Spanish at school, but it's different, isn't it, when you actually go to the place? Your GCSE Spanish just doesn't cut it. I think you've got to live there to get the vibe of how people really speak.

'Do you want to go back to Tunisia next year, Alison?' my boss asked me.

'Yes,' I said.

When I got to Tunisia again the following summer, I ran into the hotel and yelled, 'I'm back!' Back in good old *TunEnders* and this time I was in charge. I had gone from holidaymaker to team leader in about two years. Thank you!

This was the year I fell in love with a Tunisian man – and I mean deeply and passionately, love-of-my-life in love. He was the shyest waiter at the Hotel Saphir and his name was Ben.

Ben wasn't interested in me, at first. He didn't pay me any attention whatsoever, and that made me curious. I'd go and get my drinks from him. I'd smile at him. No response.

Soon I was lovestruck. What is it with this guy? It's almost as if he's ignoring me on purpose, I thought.

I became a little bit obsessed. When I asked the waiters about him, they shook their heads. 'To be honest with you, Ben wouldn't go with anybody around here. He's not one of those guys who goes out with tourists. He definitely wouldn't look at an English girl.'

I was even more hooked. I'm going to learn to speak

Tunisian, I decided. If he's not going to go out with an English girl, I'll stop speaking English to him.

I made the other waiters teach me words and phrases in Tunisian and I wrote them down in a little book. The Tunisian language is a blend of Arabic and French and I quickly picked up the basics. Then I learnt all the swear words. Suddenly I could understand more of what was going on around me, and the Tunisian people I met were even friendlier than usual, now that I was speaking their language. They were delighted. People used to say that I could speak Tunisian like a four-year-old. Like a four-year-old who swears.

One day I went up to Ben and asked him for a bottle of water, which is '*Ateeni de boosa mere*'. I'll never forget it.

He looked me in the eye and said, '*De boosa mere?*' and I said, '*De boosa mere.*'

He looked really taken aback. Then he gave me the bottle of water and smiled. Oh, my gosh, I thought, I'm in! We've made a connection.

'Where do you live?' I asked him, the next time I saw him.

He shook his head and stayed silent. He wasn't giving me anything more than a smile.

Me being me, I decided to find out for myself, so I went into the local town and asked around. I stalked him down! I know, it makes me sound like such a psycho, but I really, really liked him. 'I'm Ben's friend,' I said, showing people a photograph of him and me together at work.

It didn't take long to find his house and soon I was at his front door. 'Oh, come on in!' said his mother. That's how Tunisians are. They're lovely. They invite you in and cook for you; they just want to entertain you.

In I went and I had the best afternoon at Ben's house. I met his mum, his dad, his three sisters and his two brothers. We ate together. His sisters did my nails. They didn't have a clue who I was, really – I was just some random English girl – but they entertained me and encouraged me to take loads of photos of them and showed me photos of Ben when he was a baby.

I totally fell in love with them. They seemed to like me a lot too.

Back at work in the hotel, I went up to Ben, grinning. 'Your family are so lovely. Your mum, Jamelia, is a fantastic cook,' I said.

'You've seen my mum?'

After he'd got over the shock, he found it really funny, and I think that was what won him over. We started going out with each other. I was in Heaven. He was a lovely boyfriend in every way.

Tunisia is definitely my spirit country, along with Jamaica. They are both such wonderful places. But it's not necessarily the country itself that makes a place so special, although Jamaica and Tunisia are naturally stunning. It's how the people make me feel, how nice they are, how warm and welcoming, that makes these places so amazing.

I had a job I loved and a boyfriend I loved, and I lived in a country I loved. Nothing could go wrong, could it?

The wedding

As you can probably tell, I wasn't sure where I was going in my early twenties. I had put aside my dream of being an actor and didn't know what I was eventually going to do or where I would end up. I had faith that things would turn out all right, but sometimes I couldn't help worrying that they wouldn't.

And then something happened that showed me how important it is to make the most of life and to try to be positive and happy, no matter what . . .

It happened one night in the late nineties, when I was driving home along a country lane in my little white Fiat Uno. It was two o'clock in the morning and I'd been to a friend's barn wedding, which had been absolutely brilliant, really good fun. I had my party dress on and I'd recently lost a little bit of weight, so I was really feeling myself. Now, I don't drink, but it had been a great party, a really good night, and I'd done lots of dancing – and now I was listening to my music as I was driving along. I was on a really good vibe.

As I rounded a bend, up ahead I saw a grey car. It was upside down, with smoke rising from the bonnet.

Oh, my gosh! Has this car literally just crashed? I thought, as I pulled over.

There were two people inside the car and a young guy on the roadside yelling and clutching his leg.

I jumped out of my Fiat, my heart pounding. 'Are you okay?' I asked him breathlessly.

'My leg's hurting!' he shouted.

The fact that he was sitting up and crying told me he was going to be okay, but it was a different story when I looked into the car. The driver was slumped in the front, with his seatbelt holding him in place upside down. The guy in the back was also upside down with his seatbelt on; he was groaning in pain.

It was horrific. I was the first on the scene. I was on my own and, like most people in the nineties, I didn't have a mobile phone.

I felt so alone.

The driver was in a position that I couldn't get to, but I could see the guy in the back. 'Don't worry, I'll get some help. You'll be all right,' I told him.

On a dark country road in the middle of nowhere, I screamed for help.

A few minutes later, another car pulled up. Luckily, the driver had a car phone and called for an ambulance.

'We can't get to the guy in the front but we can reach the one in the back,' I told him. 'Let's take his seat belt off and get him out of the car.'

'No, don't touch him!' the other motorist said, looking alarmed. 'You could damage him or cripple him. Leave him upside down.'

'But we can literally help him out of the car,' I said. 'Let's at least get him the right way up. Surely he'll be better off.'

'No, don't do it. Just leave him alone.'

'Okay, then.'

He lay down on the road and tried to talk to the driver in the front of the car, while I lay down facing the guy in the back, who was still moaning and groaning. I tried to reassure him as best I could. There was petrol all over the ground and I could feel it soaking into my party dress.

It seemed like a hundred years, but after about fifteen minutes the ambulance arrived. I was so happy to let the paramedics take over. They sent me on my way and I shakily drove home at about ten miles an hour, stinking of petrol.

I was in a state of shock. Look how your life can literally change in a moment! I thought.

When I got home, I told my mum all about it and went to bed. The next morning when the newspapers came out, I read about what had happened. They were only young, those guys: one of them had stolen his dad's car and picked up his friends; they'd taken the car for a spin and written it off in the country lane where I'd found them.

The guy on the side of the road who was shouting about his leg had survived. Luckily for him, he'd been flung out of the car when it crashed. As for the other two, they had both died in hospital.

I couldn't believe it. They'd died?

The horror affected me for weeks afterwards. I kept thinking about how I'd been with these guys in their last moments, as their lives were slipping away. I couldn't help wondering if the guy in the back would have been all right if I'd lifted him out of the car. I think I probably would have gone ahead and moved him if I'd known he was going to die.

I didn't know who they were – I didn't know them from Adam – but they were young men whose lives had been tragically taken from them and I felt desperately sad for them. Look how precious life is! I kept thinking, in the days and weeks that followed.

From that moment, I decided you've got to do everything you can to enjoy life to the full. You've got to live for the moment, say yes to as many things as possible and be thankful for every day that you wake up breathing. I've never forgotten the lesson I learnt that awful night. Because you never know when life is going to be taken away from you.

5. BIG MOTHER

The next big moment in my life could so easily not have happened; it always amazes me that it did. I mean, what if it hadn't?

And my big break in life could so easily have led me nowhere, but it didn't! Oh, but what if it had?

Luckily, chance put me on the path to where I am today. Life is funny like that, because you can't always tell how big or small a moment really is . . .

Money troubles

In August 2000 I started hearing things about a new programme on Channel 4 called *Big Brother*. It was all the UK
holidaymakers in Menorca could talk about, and the English tabloid newspapers were full of it. Like most people, I
had no idea what a game-changer *Big Brother* would turn
out to be – or how hugely it would impact me. It sounded
like an interesting idea for a TV show, but a bit weird, to be
honest.

'It's a bunch of people who don't know each other, living in a house together, with cameras? What do they do all
day?'

'Eat, sleep or sit on the sofa talking rubbish,' one of the
new reps told me. She'd been watching *Big Brother* before
she came to Spain.

I couldn't picture it. 'What's interesting about it?'

'It's quite tense. They have to get each other evicted and
whoever's last out wins seventy grand.'

I still didn't get it.

A year later, *Big Brother* was on again and the second
series attracted even more press than the first had. It was
phenomenal. Every day in the papers it was '*Big Brother*
this . . .' and '*Big Brother* that . . .'

By now I was back in Tunisia and, although I was happy in my job and had a lovely boyfriend in Ben, I was in a hole financially. I'd been promoted to the role of team manager but I was in debt to the tune of four grand and there wasn't anything left over in my wage packet to pay it back. You really didn't earn very much as a holiday rep and it was stressing me out.

I was moaning about it one day when my boss said, 'Why don't you apply to go on *Big Brother 3*? You're so entertaining that people would love watching you. I reckon you'd be in with a good chance of winning that seventy grand.'

My boss was always encouraging me to try out for stuff on TV. He thought I was a natural performer. 'You think I'd have a chance at *Big Brother*?' I said thoughtfully. He had already talked me into applying to go on *Blind Date*.

I started imagining what I could do with the *Big Brother* prize money. More than anything, I wanted to be able to pay off my debt and put down a deposit on a flat. When I was in the UK, I was still staying with my mum in Birmingham and, at twenty-seven, I felt it was time to move into my own place.

Over the next few days, I looked into how to apply to *Big Brother 3*. You had to send the production company a video introducing yourself and fill in a form online. This was at a time when I didn't have a computer, so if I wanted to access the internet, I had to take the bus to the centre of town, get off at the internet café and pay by the hour for my connection. That was how I applied for *Blind Date*; that was how I applied for *Big Brother*.

'Do you want me to help you make your video for *Big Brother*?' one of the reps offered. 'I can film you on the beach if you like.'

'You know what?' I said. 'Thanks, but I think I've already got something to send them . . .'

Millennium

In the months leading up to the dawn of the year 2000 – known by absolutely everyone as 'the Millennium' – all anyone talked about was where they were going to be on New Year's Eve. That, and how cash machines were going to dish out loads of dosh on 1 January, because computers couldn't cope with the new date. Oh my gosh, people were thinking, cash machines are not going to work! But of course they did.

'Why don't you come to Newquay on the Millennium?' my friend Sarah asked me. 'Everyone here goes out in fancy dress on New Year's Eve. My mum's coming, and the rest of my family. We'll get dressed up and have a good old party out on the streets.'

It sounded fun. 'All right, then. Maybe I'll bring my video camera,' I said.

'Wicked!'

I had a bulky old camera that recorded footage on videotape. I knew it would be a pain to carry around, but decided it would be worth it to get a film of New Year's Eve 1999.

'You'll need an outfit,' Sarah added. 'Don't forget to bring one.'

A fancy-dress costume? Oh, no! I scanned my bedroom for ideas and my eyes landed on an outfit I'd been using for a Theatre In Education project.

The police had allowed us to have some old uniforms to use in a play we'd devised around police and customs officers. I had picked them up from the police uniform store in my little white Fiat Uno, with my friend Laurence.

On our way home, for a laugh, Laurence and I had put on police hats and started barking orders at people in other cars.

'Pull over! Pull over!' we shouted at them.

We were just messing around, but nobody was taking any chances. They'd pull over . . . and we'd drive off.

How naughty is that?

After a while, a car drew up next to me at a traffic light. I was just giving them the finger when the woman in the passenger seat showed a police pass and said, 'Pull over!'

'Laurence, take your hat off!' I said quickly.

We stopped the car and the police officer came to speak to me. Her eyes darted to the back seat, where I had piled up the uniforms we'd just collected.

'What are you doing with all these police uniforms?' she asked suspiciously.

'We've actually got permission to borrow them,' I said, explaining that we were using them for our Theatre In Education project.

She didn't look impressed. 'Why are you wearing them now?'

I hung my head. 'I'm so sorry, Officer. We were trying them out as something to do.'

'You know we could arrest you for impersonating a police officer, don't you?'

I felt really ashamed. 'I'm so sorry. It won't happen again, Officer.'

'Make sure it doesn't. On your way.' She walked back to her car.

'Thank you,' I said.

But a little bit of trouble like that wasn't going to stop me wearing a police uniform on New Year's Eve! No way, man! Not on the biggest night of the century.

I took my uniform to Newquay and, with my proper police hat, my high-vis jacket and my jumper with numbers on it, I genuinely looked like a bona-fide police officer. If you'd seen me, you'd have thought, Oh, my gosh, she's a police officer!

Except that I was wearing a pair of Acupuncture trainers. My trainers were the only reason you'd think, Wait a minute, she's not a police officer! A police officer would not be wearing those trainers.

Sarah dressed up as an old-fashioned glamour girl and we hit the streets of Newquay. Everyone was in fancy dress and the atmosphere was unbelievable. Very soon I realized that people weren't seeing the Acupuncture trainers and genuinely thought I was a real police officer, so I decided to be a bit naughty again.

I'd go up to someone celebrating on the street with a serious look on my face, point at the bottle they were holding and say, 'What's that?'

Instinctively, they'd shove it behind their back and mumble, 'It's a bottle of champagne.'

'Have you got a licence for it?'

'No.'

'Well, crack it open, then!'

At that, Sarah and I would burst into peals of merriment and laugh until we could barely stand up. Sarah got it all on video.

We blagged so many freebies that night. Everyone fell for the outfit! It was weird because I'd always wanted to be a police officer and in that moment I actually felt like I was one. People looked shifty when they saw me coming. 'Oh, no, it's the police! Put your champagne away!'

'Open that now!' I'd insist.

At one point, I went up to someone cooking burgers on the street and sternly asked, 'Have you got a permit to sell these burgers?'

'No.'

'Hmm. Give us one and I'll let you off,' I said.

They took me seriously – 'Ketchup with that? Pickles?' – and handed over a burger in a bun.

'And give my friend a burger, as well,' I said.

They actually gave one to Sarah too. But as we moved off to eat our food and dance in the street, someone said, 'Wait a minute! You're not a police officer! You've got Acupuncture trainers on.'

Sarah filmed it all. 'Oh, no, they've clocked the trainers. Quick, mate, run!'

Towards the end of the night, after midnight and the fireworks, when everyone was totally drunk, we started getting a little bit of hassle. 'You're not a police officer!'

people said accusingly, knocking my police hat off and squaring up to me.

Eventually, we had to run all the way home because we were getting that much abuse.

The video we made that evening was the funniest thing I'd ever seen, so in 2002 I thought, Why not send it off to *Big Brother* as my audition tape?

I filmed an introduction outside my house, while it was snowing. 'Hi, I'm Alison Hammond. Hope you enjoy my videotape.'

Then I sent it off and forgot all about it.

Left: Me in my christening clothes with my godmother, Auntie Shirley.

Below: Me on my bike on the street outside my house, loving life with my little lollipop. I'm wearing American tube socks, Nicky's shorts and his hand-me-down trainers.

Right: Me and my mates trying to look cool chilling outside some random person's house in 1991.

Left: Spending time with Uncle Paul in Jamaica when I was eighteen.

Me, in my prime, twenty-one years old, after I'd gone on a diet, before I discovered eyebrow threading.

My mum doing her classic side pose with my dad's truck in Jamaica,
before he put the lovely little lamb in the back.

My mum, chilling outside our house. Even though she's wearing her 'house and garden dress' for pottering around in, she's still looking fine with her gold rings and cool shades.

My dad, me and my half-brother, Ali.

My first Winnebago, when I played a police officer in *The Locksmith* with Warren Clarke. The make-up artist made me look absolutely stunning – I had the brightest red lipstick you've ever seen – but I was in a very serious scene where Warren Clarke had to cry his eyes out, so it was the wrong look completely.

Me in Tunisia on the rickety old stage, after I became a team leader, with a load of tourists who can't keep their hands off me!

Waiting for Santa to arrive on Christmas Day at the hotel in Tunisia. I'm all smiles, but later on I was crying my eyes out.

Above: On the indoor stage in Tunisia with Dean, another entertainer.

Left: With my school friends Lorraine, Louise, Debs and Miranda on one of our regular nights out.

Paradise lost

While I was in England for a couple of weeks seeing my mum, I was called for an audition at *Big Brother*'s production company. 'We loved your video! Will you come in and see us?' I went along and had a chat about me and my life. I didn't for a minute think I'd get it.

I flew back to Tunisia a day earlier than planned because I was missing Ben. Things were going really well between us and I was madly in love with him, so as soon as I'd landed, I went to his house, planning to surprise him. But he wasn't at home. His family said he was at the beach so I went off to find him there.

The beach was packed and it took me a while to find him. I couldn't wait to see his face when he spotted me – he was going to be so surprised! But when I finally located him, I stopped dead in my tracks. My boyfriend was cuddling and kissing another girl.

I'd always thought there would be a massive drama if I ever caught someone I loved with another woman. I imagined I'd react by going over, slapping his face and screaming, 'How dare you?'

But it wasn't like that at all. Instead, I carried on watching – and that was the worst thing about it. I sat on the beach, mesmerized by how Ben was kissing and touching this girl, how he was holding her face. That's exactly what he does to me, I thought.

It was torture. I was absolutely devastated. I stayed and watched until they left the beach. They didn't see me as they walked away hand in hand. I went on sitting there and, as the shock wore off, I realized he'd probably been doing this with other women all along.

That evening, Ben came over while I was on the stage getting things ready for the evening cabaret. 'Alison, you're back!' He looked really happy to see me. 'Why haven't you come and said hello?'

'I came to say hello on the beach today,' I said. 'You were there. I saw you.'

His face changed. 'You saw me on the beach?'

I could barely look at him. 'Yeah, I saw you on the beach. Did you have a nice time?'

He looked upset. 'Listen, I knew her before I knew you,' he said. 'She was here on holiday again and came to find me. I didn't know what to do. I was just being nice.'

'You were snogging her face off!'

'Come on! Would you want me to be horrible to her?'

'No, you weren't horrible. I could see you weren't horrible at all. You were having a great time.'

He took a step towards me. 'Can we talk?'

I stepped away from him. 'There's nothing to talk about, is there?'

'Let's talk. I'll come round to your room later,' he pleaded.

But I had made up my mind. 'No, don't come. Let's leave it.'

That was it. It was over.

His sister came to find me the next day. 'Ben is angry with us for telling you he was at the beach yesterday,' she said. 'He doesn't want to break up with you and he's blaming us. We're so sorry.'

'It's not your fault,' I said.

'Will you forgive him?'

I shook my head sadly. Although I really loved Ben, I couldn't go back. When you see your boyfriend kissing someone else – and kissing them the same way they kiss you – it's too upsetting. It was the end of our relationship.

It taught me something: I realized you need to be careful when you have a love affair abroad, because the men you meet in touristy places are often having affairs with lots of other women. Now I know this sounds like a generalization, but you have to remember that I was living there for quite a while so I saw a lot of women who were cheated on. I thought I was different because I was out in Tunisia for long periods of time, but I shouldn't have expected Ben to be faithful to me when I wasn't there. He was young. All these opportunities were coming his way and he had his life to live. Almost the saddest part of it for me was that I couldn't see his family any more. But that's life, isn't it? I stopped wanting to be in Tunisia. It wasn't the country I was attached to as much as the people, and now that I couldn't spend time with the people I loved, I felt I had no reason to stay.

Maybe, without being totally conscious of it, I was getting ready to start a new chapter in my life. Maybe I could sense that something Big was coming my way.

Big Brother

It was an organic, natural process that led me to appear in *Big Brother*, a show I had never actually watched. It was almost accidental. Take my audition tape, for instance. Sarah and I just filmed it for a laugh. I wasn't thinking at the time that it was going to unlock the door to my future career.

Back in Tunisia, I heard from them again. 'Can you come back to England? We want to continue talking to you with regard to *Big Brother 3*.'

I flew to England, went to London for an audition and caught the train to Birmingham. No sooner had I got back than they asked me to return to London for another audition, and then another – and although they kept calling me back, I didn't seem to be getting anywhere. I don't think I've got this, I thought.

Everything went quiet and I flew back to Tunisia. A couple of days later, I had a call from a producer at *Blind Date*. Now, I had always wanted to go on *Blind Date* and they were offering me the role of one of the choosers. Wicked, I thought. I'm going to meet Cilla Black!

Two days later, I had a call from one of the executives at *Big Brother*, saying, 'Alison, where are you? We want you to go into the *Big Brother* house next week.'

'Are you serious?' I yelped.

'Absolutely serious. Do you still want to do it?'

'Can I call you back?'

It was a bizarre sliding-doors moment. Both shows were filming at the same time, so it was yes to one and no to the other – but which? I knew what I was getting into with *Blind Date*, but I hadn't watched *Big Brother 1* or *2* because I was always away when it was on TV.

I've always wanted to go on *Blind Date* and maybe I'll meet my future husband! I thought, But you know what? I've got a four-thousand-pound debt I need to pay off. Let's try to win this game show.

Shallow Alison: I chose money over love! I went to speak to my manager. 'I'm so, so sorry about this, because I know I've been messing you around, but *Big Brother* want me to go into the house next week.'

'Go for it, Al, go for it,' he said.

It was a leap into the unknown, but I would have taken any chance to pay off my debt.

I went back to *Big Brother* and said yes. 'Fantastic,' the producer said. 'You understand, don't you, that you mustn't tell anybody you're going into the house?'

'I understand,' I said, trying not to smile, because I knew I wouldn't be able to keep this sort of news secret.

Airtours flew me home to the UK straight away. They were so good to me. Back in Birmingham, there were posters up all over town advertising the third series of *Big Brother*.

If I saw someone looking at a *Big Brother* billboard on the street, I'd say, 'I'm going in there, you know.'

'Yeah, sure you are.'

'No, I am!'

I was too excited to keep such a big secret to myself and I told my mum, my mates, all my friends at work and everybody else I knew. Tell me a sad secret or something personal and I won't tell a soul. But I can't help blurting out happy news – and I didn't think any of my friends or colleagues would call the press.

In the week before I went into the *Big Brother* house, I did a little bit of research and watched a few old *Big Brother* episodes. This is a weird show, I thought. It seemed like a load of rubbish to me. I couldn't imagine anyone wanting to watch it. Just go in and be yourself, I thought. I can do that. It won't be hard.

I didn't know the show or understand the premise, so I didn't go in with a game plan. Since I'm not really a controversial sort of person, I thought it would be easy, just a question of getting on with the other housemates.

A few days before we were due to go into the *Big Brother* house, a story broke about Jade Goody, who was also in *Big Brother 3*, and the producers contacted us to say that we had to go into lockdown.

Considering the number of people I've told, I can't believe it's not my fault! I thought with relief.

In later years, they started locking housemates down for weeks before they went into the *Big Brother* house – they even sent them to another country to lock them down. My housemates and I had to stay in a hotel for four days and that was enough for me. Lockdown is a more familiar term to us now than it was then (sadly!) and this was an extreme form of it: they take your phone away; you have to stay in the hotel room; you've got a chaperone who comes in with your food and drink, who stays with you all the time until you go to sleep. You can't contact anyone; you can't ring out on the hotel phone. It was terrible: I couldn't speak to my mum! You have no outside contact whatsoever. Imagine being locked down in a different country, on top of all that. I wouldn't like it at all.

What I didn't know, while I was shut up in my hotel room, was that there were reporters outside my house in Birmingham asking my mum about me. They were even going round to the neighbours' houses to ask questions.

At one point my mum popped her head out of our little bathroom window at the top of the house and said, 'No comment!'

I just love the thought of her doing that. It really tickles me.

Breaking things

At the start of our *Big Brother* adventure, we were told, 'Don't break anything, because you will have to pay for it.'

Maybe I should have thought harder about agreeing to be on the show, because I'm one of the klutziest people in the world. I should have known I was going to break something – in fact, I should have put a special clause in my contract about it because I'm always breaking things. All my friends know me for it. Literally, they will put me in a room with a glass and then count to five, knowing that by the time they've stopped counting the glass will be broken. That's how klutzy I am. I've probably broken about a million pounds' worth of stuff in my lifetime.

Alison's top-dollar klutzy moments

Klutzy moment #1
In *Big Brother*, I broke a picnic bench. An actual picnic bench.

Klutzy moment #2
When I was younger, I climbed up onto a garage roof and fell through the roof onto a car.

Klutzy moment #3

I rocked up to a desert restaurant and sat in a plastic chair. Instead of it actually holding my weight, it melted, like plasticine.

Klutzy moment #4

On my first day of filming on *This Morning*, it was going really well until I went to the Ladies and unfortunately dropped my radio microphone into the toilet and broke it. The sound man was not happy.

Klutzy moment #5

I did an Instagram Live making mini pancakes and it was going really well until I accidentally knocked the frying pan off the counter and onto the floor. It was live; it was embarrassing. I went to pick up the pan and the pancakes and discovered I'd broken one of my floor tiles, which I was mortified about. Do you know what? That floor tile is still broken.

It's always been the same. When my mum was an auxiliary nurse and worked at night, our neighbours, Dawn and Barry, used to have me to sleep over. They were really great neighbours, really helpful to my mum – they'd check up on her and offer to help out in all sorts of ways. Their kids were much younger than me, but we got on well and I liked going next door.

One day, when I was about twelve, I was in Dawn and Barry's living room watching the children's TV programme

Super Gran, when I got up on their table and jumped off, pretending to fly. Can I just say here that we were all messing around? But, yes, I had to go one step further and actually get onto the table and be Super Gran. And with that, the table buckled underneath me, fell over and the corner smashed onto five-year-old Anthony's head and cut it open. Chaos! Panic! Poor Anthony started screaming and his mum and dad came rushing in. There was blood everywhere – I'd never seen so much blood in my life and Barry was yelling that his son was going to die. I thought I'd killed Anthony. I felt so bad.

Dawn and Barry called an ambulance and took Anthony to hospital, where he got stitched up and, thank God, was all right. What was nice was that none of the family ever told my mum about it so I didn't get into trouble. Not even for breaking their table. As I said, they were really nice neighbours.

The other day I bumped into Anthony and he lifted up his fringe to show me the scar on his hairline. No hair grows there to this day. It's so awful to think I did that to him!

I was devastated. 'Have you forgiven me yet?' I asked.

'Yeah, course I have,' he said.

Nothing as awful as that ever happened again, but I went on breaking things. The time I went along with my mum to one of the Tupperware parties she hosted at a client's house wasn't great. I didn't really want to go because Mum always did the same party games and came out with the same banter when she did these parties at people's houses, so I found it quite boring. I'd do anything to get out of staying and hearing the same thing over again, even if it meant playing with random kids in the street.

This particular evening, there was a load of children at the house and we all went outside and played football. I was really enjoying myself, thinking, This is brilliant, man! when I slogged the ball to try to score a goal. It curved in and hit the very window of the room where my mum was doing her Tupperware party. As I heard the glass shatter, my heart dropped like a stone in my chest. Oh, my gosh, Mum is going to go mad!

Mum had to pay for a replacement window so she didn't make any money that night. I felt absolutely terrible about it, but Mum wasn't too angry. She accepted that I'm accident prone. It's just a part of me.

Sometimes Mum took me with her on her rounds when she was a community nurse. She'd drive around, visiting different people's houses, only ever going in for about ten minutes. I never knew what she was doing because she never took me in with her. I'd just sit in the car and listen to music as I waited for her to come out.

One day, when I was on her rounds with her, I was in the front of the car with my feet up on the dashboard, tapping my toes on the window to the music and really enjoying myself. A Michael Jackson song came on and I was really getting into it, when the next thing I knew the windscreen had cracked right across the middle. Oh, no! What shall I do? What shall I say? I started to panic, knowing my mum would be furious with me.

She came out, saw the crack and said, 'What's happened? What's going on?'

'Mum, you're not going to believe this,' I said, making it up on the spot. 'A car drove past and flicked up a stone that hit the window and it just cracked.'

'Oh, Alison, that's terrible. Are you all right?'

If in doubt, lie! It was mischievous of me, but I didn't want to admit to my mistake, to be honest with you. I didn't want to get into trouble – and I got away with it, thankfully.

But now I was in a situation where there was no getting away with anything. I was on no account allowed to break anything in the *Big Brother* house without paying for it – and I was already in debt. We weren't being paid to appear on *Big Brother*, but we were getting thirty pounds a day to cover our expenses, and I was going to need it when I came out, if I didn't win the prize money.

I would have to make sure I was very, very careful.

The *BB* house

People often ask, 'What was it really like in the *Big Brother* house?'

I say, 'Did you watch it?'

They say, 'Yeah.'

And I say, 'That's exactly what it's like, but longer and more boring.'

The next time you watch *Big Brother*, if it's ever on again, imagine that you're inside the TV. That's what it's like being on *Big Brother*. It's the only way I can describe it.

I went into the *Big Brother* house on 24 May 2002. Afterwards, Davina McCall made a big thing out of the fact that I packed twenty-six pairs of knickers to take in with me, but I don't know why it was even news. There's nothing worse than not having a clean pair of pants, is there? I didn't know how long I was staying and wasn't sure whether I'd always have access to a washing-machine, so I figured it was better to be safe than sorry.

I was really nervous before the show, but I enjoyed my time on *Big Brother*, as it happens. For me, it felt like going on holiday with a group of new people. I think it made a difference that I didn't really understand how the show worked, because if I'd studied it beforehand, I might have over-thought it. Instead, I went in and had fun just being myself. I had a couple of down days, but apart from that, it was an amazing experience.

As I'd just come back from Tunisia, I slotted happily into the role of the housemates' holiday rep. I had lots of games up my sleeve to keep people entertained – and, believe me, you had to have something to pass the time because being in *Big Brother* really is quite boring. You're in this massive house, but you can't go anywhere except the garden. You're told what to do. You're told when to go to bed. You're told when to wake up. You're told what foods you're allowed to have and you have to plan your house-hold budget. It's difficult. On the upside, it was lovely sunny weather while I was there, and they had a pool, so at least you could get into your bikini or swimming costume and go for a dip.

I'm not going to lie: you do feel a bit trapped some-times, because you are trapped. If you don't want to be in there, you can leave whenever you want, but while you're there, you are locked in and there's security everywhere. Not only that, but the cameras see everything. Imagine the bathroom: you're literally being seen all the time. I couldn't go to the toilet for the first five days. I just couldn't relax.

On the fifth day, I thought, Do you know what? I'm just going to have to forget about the cameras and go to the toilet.

Actually, you don't forget that they're there: you just get used to them. Anyway, the editors don't really concentrate on the cameras in the bathroom unless people speak to each other in there. It's only then that they pay attention. And when I went into the gallery after the whole thing was finished, I noticed that the shower camera and the toilet camera monitors were very small.

There were a lot of different personalities in the house and I did my best to get on with them all. Obviously not everybody is going to gel in that situation. In the house with me were people like Jonny Regan, Sandy Cumming, Adele Roberts, Lee Davey, PJ Ellis, Alex Sibley, Kate Lawler and Spencer Smith – all very different characters.

There wasn't anyone I disliked and I made a few lifelong friends – result! Me and Kate Lawler are really close and I'm so proud of everything that she's become, especially her radio career. I'm mates with PJ as well, and still speak to Jonny, who's a photographer and smashing it in County Durham.

Although Kate won *Big Brother 3* – and she deserved to win, because she was the nicest person you could possibly meet – maybe the surprise star of the show was Jade Goody. When Jade came out of the show, she became a superstar. She was absolutely loved by the public. And Jade was amazing, actually. She was sometimes misunderstood, but deep down, she was a sweet woman and I got on well with her.

It really upset me when I found out a few years later that Jade wasn't well. It hurt my heart, and when she died, I was devastated, partly because Jade was the first young person I knew who had passed. Loads of newspapers contacted me, wanting to do interviews about her death, but I kept saying no because I didn't think it was right to speak about her. It just seemed crass. It was a weird time and I didn't like it.

She's gone. Let her rest in peace, I thought.

Food

I was happy to make fun of myself while I was in the *Big Brother* house. From the moment I arrived, I had a laugh about my size and weight. The other housemates seemed to find it funny – and it made my weight a non-issue, to the point where no one would mention it, because I'd got in there first.

I made little jokes about it all the time: for instance, I'd eat my meal and say, 'Oh, I couldn't eat another thing!' and then put a little spoonful of something else in my mouth. It really used to make Jonny laugh. I did it at every meal: I'd finish eating and say, 'No more, thanks – I'm absolutely stuffed,' and then pop in another spoonful, just for the lols.

I really missed Chinese food while I was in the *Big Brother* house. We did have it one night and it was delicious – I got up the next morning looking forward to eating the leftovers. But when I got down to the kitchen, I couldn't find them anywhere.

'Where's the Chinese from last night? There was loads left over,' I said.

'Oh, we chucked it away,' someone said.

'Are you absolutely joking? You've thrown away all that lovely leftover Chinese food?'

They didn't get it. 'Yeah.'

I was mortified. 'What a waste! We could have had that for breakfast.'

At home, I'll always have my Chinese from the night before for breakfast. I'll put it in the fridge and the next day I'll reheat it and eat it. Maybe it's something to do with where I came from, but there's no way I'd throw out leftover food.

One of the freezers in the house accidentally turned itself off in the middle of the night, and in the morning, a week's worth of food had started to defrost, including a tub of Ben & Jerry's ice cream. In order not to waste it, I thought, I might as well eat it for breakfast.

I got a few funny looks for eating ice cream at that time of day, but what other option was there? It would have been ruined otherwise. So I smashed the Ben & Jerry's. Waste not, want not.

The table

From the start, I was scared to go into the diary room. I tried to avoid it as much as I could because it felt like being called in to speak to the head teacher at school.

I only went when they specifically said, 'Alison Hammond, come to the diary room.'

Those words filled me with absolute dread. Oh, no! I'd think. What have I done now?

Not having watched *Big Brother 1* or *2*, I truly hadn't done enough research, but I get it now. You're supposed to use Big Brother as a diary or a log book. You're supposed to tell Big Brother if you don't like somebody, or you feel down. But I kept everything to myself and that's not the way to play *Big Brother*. You've got to open up with your emotions.

I kept thinking about what they'd said: 'If you break something, you have to pay for it.'

I don't know why they tell you that because it puts the fear of God into you. I wasn't too worried about the odd glass or plate, but when somebody started joking that I'd broken a chair, two loungers and a bed, it made me really nervous. And then disaster struck.

Me and Kate Lawler were standing on a picnic bench in

the garden. We were trying to look over the top of the fence and see what was going on outside. We had been out of contact with the world for two weeks now and were missing the Queen's Golden Jubilee and the World Cup – not that I was particularly bothered about the football, but it still felt weird to be so isolated. People outside kept trying to get messages to us: you'd have planes flying over trailing banners that said, 'Good luck, Jade,' or 'Don't trust Adele.' They'd throw tennis balls into the garden with little notes on them and, suddenly, Big Brother would say, 'Do not go in the garden!' and we'd have to stay inside while someone went out to retrieve the tennis balls.

So it was thrilling to discover that, standing on the picnic table, me and Kate could see people over the fence. We got so excited that we jumped up to get a better view. Big mistake. When I landed on the table again, it snapped and buckled beneath me.

Time stopped. Kate and I froze. Oh, no, I'm going to have to pay for this, I thought in horror.

What made it ten times worse was that it didn't appear to be a normal, cheap picnic bench. It was expensive-looking. Perhaps it was even mahogany and worth a lot of money. I'm going to have to give back all the expenses I've made in here and take out another loan to pay them back for the table, I thought glumly.

I went straight to the diary room. 'I've done something really, really bad, but it was an accident,' I told Big Brother. 'I think I've just broken the outside table by jumping on it.'

Now, I knew very well that I'd broken the table. I absolutely had broken the table. So, by saying, '*I think* I've just

159

broken the table,' I was just trying to worm my way out of it, because I hadn't got the money to pay for it and was mortified. 'I'm really sorry. What do you want me to do? I could probably bend it back,' I added desperately, even though there was no chance of that. I can't believe I've done this! I thought. I was so disappointed in myself.

Can you imagine how relieved I felt when I heard that I didn't have to pay for the table, after all? I was ready to have a party when I got that news. I literally jumped for joy – but on solid ground, this time. (I wasn't taking any more risks!)

Eviction

I got evicted from the *Big Brother* house on day fourteen. Gutted. I burst into tears. I really didn't want to go.

Kate Lawler was in tears as well. 'I haven't known you for long, but I really love you, man,' she said, when we heard I'd been nominated for eviction, a couple of days earlier. Now I was leaving and she seemed almost as gutted as I was.

If I'd understood more about how *Big Brother* works, I don't think I'd have been so upset to hear that I'd been nominated. At the time I wondered, What have I done wrong? because I didn't realize that people don't necessarily vote out the person they don't like. For instance, I think Spencer nominated me because I was sleeping in the double bed. He didn't necessarily dislike me: he just wanted my double bed; and it might also have been because he fancied Kate Lawler and I kept sleeping in the double bed with Kate.

'Don't get upset,' I told Kate, when Big Brother announced I was leaving. 'I am so not upset about the situation. Think about it: if I go out, my family's going to be there. How cool is that?'

As it happened, I was really missing my family. I hadn't told anyone that my three-year-old niece, Jasmine, wasn't very well and had gone into hospital. This was the little girl I'd seen being born, when I'd stayed that day to be a birth partner to Saundra and laugh at her American accent. Everyone in the family was worried sick about Jasmine and I'd had serious doubts about whether I should even go into the *Big Brother* house.

'Do you definitely want me to do this show? Because if Jasmine's not well, I'd rather be with you,' I'd said to Saundra.

'No, go and do *Big Brother*. Jasmine can watch it in hospital and it will keep her spirits up to see her Auntie Ali on TV,' she'd insisted.

When I left the house, Saundra told me that while she was in hospital, Jasmine watched *Big Brother* every day from her hospital bed. Lots of the nurses and doctors who were treating her watched it with her and she was able to tell them that her Auntie was on the television. It definitely boosted her morale, poor little thing, and I was pleased that I'd been able to help in some way.

Despite my assurances to Kate, though, I was mortified that I'd been evicted. After I'd done my final interview with Davina and given her a load of cuddles, I went to speak to the *Big Brother* psychologist. 'Alison, you have done yourself no harm whatsoever,' he said calmly. 'And this is the perfect time for you to come out because things are changing from tomorrow.'

He explained that the following day they were going to divide the house into rich side–poor side. 'You would have really struggled if you'd ended up on the poor side,' he said.

I thought about it later and decided he was right. I would

have hated being on miserable rations, in a horrible room, on the poor side! I would have had to go on the rich side – or walk out.

Having said that, the side you were allocated was decided by shooting basketball hoops – and I would have absolutely smashed that because, as you know, I was quite a sporty kid. I reckon I would have got on to the rich side, without a doubt.

However, I had been evicted. I wasn't playing any more and had to go home.

At least I finally had a chance to watch *Big Brother*! I followed it avidly after I was evicted – it was extra fascinating because I knew all the housemates personally.

'Oh, man. I get it now,' I said, slapping my head as I began to understand what it was all about and how to play the game. But by then it was too late. Or so I thought.

6. ON THE RED CARPET

I wasn't prepared for the highs and lows of life after *Big Brother*. For a while, the future looked rather bleak and I was feeling low. But I was lucky: another opportunity came along and I took it, only to klutz things up again in true Alison style! Somehow I managed to cling on, though, and as time went on, a whole new world of fun and laughter started to open up to me.

My new life

My life changed from the moment I left the *Big Brother* house. Instead of going home to Birmingham, I stayed in a hotel in London for two weeks and did non-stop interviews with press and TV. I even had a team of people to look after me. Amazing!

Little did I know when I broke the picnic bench in the garden with Kate how funny people would find it – or how hilarious I would appear when I went into the diary room to confess. Who'd have thought that in that moment I'd become really popular with *Big Brother* viewers? At the time, I was consumed by the fear that I was going to have to pay for the broken bench. I wasn't thinking about how I was coming across on TV; I was purely worrying about money.

Everyone I met when I got out of the *Big Brother* house kept going on about the picnic bench. 'Comedy gold,' they were saying. 'You made the whole country laugh.'

I didn't realize how much it had impacted people until a couple of guys on my team took me shopping on Oxford Street, two days later. With days of interviews stretching ahead of me and no time to wash my clothes, I'd decided it would be easier to buy some new bits and pieces. Bad move. Within seconds of getting out of the car, I was mobbed. I literally could not move for people crowding around me. 'Alison! Alison! Can I have an autograph? Can I have a picture?'

It was crazy. Everywhere I looked, people were shouting, waving and yelling my name. They were even hanging out of the windows of the buildings, calling out, 'Up here, Alison! We love you!'

I was completely taken aback. 'This *Big Brother* is big stuff, isn't it?' I said to one of the guys.

'Huge!' he said.

There was no social media in 2002 and to see someone off the TV was a big thing. Nowadays, with Instagram and Twitter, you get to see into people's lives, but the public knew nothing about me when I came out of *Big Brother* and they wanted to know more: 'Who is this big Black woman with her dreads?' People wanted a piece of Alison, even though I'd only been on the television for two weeks.

As the sea of strangers in Oxford Street pressed in on me, I stood by the car, trying to smile and be polite. It was a strange situation. There was no point trying to get to the shops now – there was just no way I would have made it through the crowd.

'Come on, I think we'd better get you out of here; it's too much,' my guys said.

The street was now so crammed with people that I could hardly breathe. It was overwhelming. 'Oh my God! Is my life going to be like this for ever?' I thought.

Short answer: no. When you come out of *Big Brother*, you're famous for a week and then it's the next person to get evicted who gets mobbed when they try to go to the shops. The interviews end. The TV shows don't need you any more. The focus shifts elsewhere.

It was a major anticlimax for me. How could it not be? The build-up had been immense, my time in the house intense; I'd had a week of being in the spotlight and now . . . nothing. 'I suppose I'll just go back to work, then,' I thought, feeling completely deflated.

I phoned up the managers of the cinema where I had a part-time job and asked if I could come back. 'Sorry, it's too soon,' they said. 'You're too famous now. It would be too distracting if you came back to work for us now.'

I didn't think Airtours would want me to go back to Tunisia either. Suddenly the future looked very bleak. If I wasn't going to be able to work or live my life normally, what would I do? I still had thousands of pounds of debt to worry about.

'Oh dear, did I do the right thing going into *Big Brother*?' I asked myself. 'Did I make the right choice?'

Without any prospect of finding work for the moment, there was nothing for it but to sign on at my local dole office back in Birmingham. But even that wasn't simple. Not wanting anyone to recognize me, I went in disguise, in a tracksuit with my hoody up and dark glasses covering my eyes. I went in, filled in all the forms, handed them over and made my way out, thinking I'd got away with it. Just as I was leaving, the security guard at the door said, 'Thanks, Alison, see you soon.'

He can't have known for sure it was me – I was covered up from head to toe – but I stupidly said, 'Bye,' – and with that one word I blew my cover, just like Gordon Jackson in *The Great Escape*.

For the next couple of months, I lay low at home, wondering what on earth I was going to do with the rest of my life.

'Don't worry, Al, something will turn up,' my mum reassured me. 'You're exactly where you're supposed to be right now. Just have faith that things will get better soon.'

'Okay,' I said. As long as I had my mum, I knew everything would be all right.

Then, out of the blue, Richard, my agent at the time, phoned me.

'Alison? I've had a call from *This Morning* and they'd like you to go to London for a meeting,' he said.

A producer had seen a tape of my *Big Brother* eviction and thought, 'Alison clearly likes her food. Let's get her in for a chat about our new diet strand.'

The next thing I knew, I was presenting a weekly section about healthy weight loss on *This Morning*! It was only a three-month contract and I had no idea where it would lead, but it was the break I needed.

'Didn't I tell you that something would turn up?' my mum said, when I rang her with the good news.

'Yes, Mum, you did,' I said happily.

The microphone

It was coming up to Christmas and the end of my three-month contract with *This Morning* so I was wondering what I was going to do next. I remembered being interviewed by Dermot O'Leary on *Big Brother's Little Brother*, the week after I'd come out of the *Big Brother* house. I'd made him laugh at something silly, and he'd said, 'Alison, you should really go into children's television presenting.'

Could kids' TV be the way forward for me? Or would I just go back to working at my local cinema?

I was thinking things over when I had a phone call from one of the *This Morning* producers asking me to interview George Clooney on the red carpet of a film premiere, along with the other stars of the movie.

Me? Interview George Clooney?

'When?' I asked.

'Tomorrow.'

'Are you sure you want me to do it? I've never done anything like this before.'

Up until this point in my life, I hadn't met a lot of celebrities. There had been Muhammad Ali, who had won me over with his magic tricks, and Pat Roach, the strongest man in Britain, who was in business with my dad. My mum had been good friends with the TV chef Rustie Lee since they were kids, and I had fond memories of going to Rustie's Caribbean restaurant in Birmingham with my mum and dad. Finally, I'd eaten Chinese takeaway with the members of the reggae-pop group Musical Youth round at one of their mums' houses when they were at the height of their fame in the early eighties, which had left me speechless with awe and wonder. (Well, I was only eight.)

As I made my way to the premiere of George Clooney's directorial debut, *Confessions of a Dangerous Mind*, in Leicester Square, I kept remembering how tongue-tied I'd been meeting Kelvin and Michael from Musical Youth. The thought of now interviewing all these film stars I'd seen on TV was nerve-racking: what if nothing came out of my mouth when I tried to ask them a question?

'Just relax and be yourself,' my director said.

It was the best advice he could have given me.

On the red carpet, I chatted to a few of the celebrities and it was all going fine. Then this big Hollywood superstar rocked up. George Clooney. This was it. My first big interview.

I asked a couple of questions and it went really well. I was absolutely buzzing afterwards. I've just interviewed George Clooney! I thought. This is crazy.

A few minutes later, I saw him walking back down the carpet. Great! He's coming back! I thought. I might as well ask him a few more questions.

What I didn't know was that, once you've interviewed someone at an event, you DO NOT get to interview them again. So we were at cross-purposes as he walked towards me – and when I lifted my microphone to ask him a question I accidentally smashed him in the face with it.

Oh, no! No, no, no, no, no!

He swerved out of the way. 'I'm so sorry!' I said, mortified.

I was so incredibly embarrassed, but he took it in good humour and started laughing. Phew! Right then and there, I decided that George Clooney was an absolute gem.

Meeting him again a couple of years later only confirmed to me what an all-round nice guy he is. We were at a sit-down junket in a hotel and he said, 'You're that girl who hit me in the face with a microphone!'

'Oh, my God, you remember?'

He smiled. 'Yeah, I remember.'

You can't get away with anything with these Hollywood celebs, I thought. It really made me laugh.

I thought he was amazing, so professional and so nice, and he could charm everyone, men and women alike. I think we all fell in love with George Clooney at that junket. He's the sort of guy everyone likes and wants to be around.

'If there were no rules, what would you get up to?' I asked him.

'I think you know what I'd be up to,' he said. 'I think everybody in this room would be up to it too. What would you be up to?'

'I'd run my fingers through your hair,' I said.

'That would be hard to do because I just bought it,' he joked, pretending that he was wearing a wig. 'Go on, then.'

And so I did. I ran my fingers through George Clooney's hair. What a moment that was!

Celebrity interviewer

After my run-in with George Clooney and the microphone, I didn't expect to get any more work interviewing celebrities. But people seemed to think it was hilarious that I'd nearly knocked out the biggest film star in the world.

After that, every now and then, I was sent along to red carpets and hotels to meet film and music stars. I kept in mind my director's advice and tried to relax and be myself, and it seemed to work well. People kept saying, 'That was fantastic! You're so funny.'

What are they finding funny? I wondered, because I wasn't actually trying to be funny. Then I'd watch it back. Ah, I get it. That is quite funny, but it could have been funnier. Now I know how to make the next one funnier.

The key was watching myself back, which I know a lot of people don't do, but I find it helps me see where I'm going wrong or if I could do something a little bit different. My name's Hammond, so I can ham anything up.

After that, I challenged myself to see how funny I could make things, and that's what I got off on. I realized that if I had fun, the viewers would too. How much fun could we have? It wasn't difficult because I wasn't acting and didn't have to learn any lines. It was literally me being me – and people were enjoying seeing me for who I was.

Me being me was enough! It was such a nice feeling. This is easy! I thought.

I didn't work every day: I'd have a couple of days one week and maybe one or two the next, but I was more than contented to be working ad hoc.

One of my earliest big interviews was when I met Britney Spears around the time she was releasing her fourth album, *In the Zone*, in 2003. I was flown to New York to meet her – yay! I love New York.

I was happy and relaxed when I got to Trump Tower, where the interview was taking place, but when I saw the security detail on the floor where I was interviewing Britney, I started getting nervous. Fortunately, when I finally got into the interviewing room, there was Britney, smiling sweetly. She was a breath of fresh air and I relaxed.

Britney seemed to find me funny so at the end of the interview I sprang a little surprise on her.

'I've always wanted to be one of your backing dancers,' I said, 'so this is the ideal opportunity for me to audition for you and for you to give me your honest reaction. Is that all right, everybody? Britney, you might want to use some of these moves in your next show.'

'Yeah, I'm so open. I can't wait!' she said.

I showed her some of my moves and gave her a running commentary: 'Punch-punch, round-round, roll down the body, roll down the body . . .' I was really going for it. 'What do you think?' I asked her, when I'd finished my routine.

'That was great!' she said, beaming. 'I love the punch-punch part. Do that again!'

I went through it once more and asked her if I'd made it through the audition.

'Well . . . yes!' she said hesitantly.

And that was my first interview with Britney. It was good fun and set me up to interview her several times in the following years, I'm glad to say, because I always like seeing her. She's a lovely girl with a great sense of humour: it's been good every time.

I've interviewed lots of fabulous female stars and I've loved meeting every one of them: Oprah Winfrey, Renée Zellweger, Mariah Carey, Sandra Bullock, Glenn Close, Gloria Estefan, Reese Witherspoon, Julie Andrews, Jennifer Aniston . . . all amazing women! I'm not saying Beyoncé was my favourite, but she has always been a heroine of mine so I was thrilled to meet her in 2008, before the release of her third solo album, *I Am . . . Sasha Fierce.*

'Haven't I met you before?' she said.

Beyoncé recognized me! I couldn't believe it: I had interviewed her five years earlier, on the red carpet at the film premiere of *Charlie's Angels.* Actually, it was a pink carpet, but did she really remember it? I'll never know.

Now we were in a hotel room and I was so in awe of her that I was worried about saying the wrong thing. Fortunately she was really lovely and easy to chat to.

The first single off her album was 'If I Were A Boy', so I took that title and ran with it.

'If you were a boy, how would you do things differently?' I asked her. 'Because I know I wouldn't leave the toilet seat up.'

'I wouldn't either,' she agreed.

'I wouldn't be scratching my nether regions in front of me. I wouldn't be doing that.'

She laughed. 'No, it's not cool. I would definitely want to be a guy that is faithful and a good man and kind of show other men how to do it right, you know what I mean?'

I liked the way she raised the tone so effortlessly. It was admirable. I decided to surprise her with some rumours and gossip. 'I've heard that you're going to have an extra member in Destiny's Child, and apparently it's me,' I said.

'Yeah, but you're not supposed to tell anybody yet,' she replied, in whispered tones. Gotta love her!

When I ran out of questions, I got out the Connect 4 and challenged her to a game. I know – resourceful! She was totally up for it and beat me hands down. I'm usually unbeatable so I blame it on the nerves: I couldn't concentrate because I kept thinking, I'm playing Connect 4 with Beyoncé and she's absolutely beautiful. This is a dream come true.

First impressions

Funny things always seemed to happen when I was waiting around to interview people. Wait, did I say 'funny'? Actually, I meant 'embarrassing'. I'm thinking of the time I went along to a junket for a Ben Stiller movie at the Dorchester Hotel, which is one of the most exclusive hotels in London. It's an absolutely amazing place: you've got all your Ferraris outside; the food is really expensive and a cup of tea is about ten quid. For some reason the interviews were running late that day, but what's great about these junkets is that they provide you with really nice food and drink while you're waiting. If it's a big film, they might really go for it and put out a spread of salad, chicken, cake, muffins, biscuits and lovely quality bottled water.

I helped myself to some salad and a drink and prepared myself for a long wait. It was fast turning into an afternoon out with a bunch of other journalists. 'Do you want to come and wait outside the room?' someone asked me eventually.

'Why not?' I said, thinking it would make a change of scene, if nothing else.

So now I was standing in the corridor outside the room where I was going to interview Ben Stiller. I was quite tired after all the waiting around and I leant against the wall for support.

After a few moments, I started to hear a buzzing sound. It was really quite loud. What is that? I thought.

Everyone in the corridor was looking around, thinking the same thing. What is that weird sound?

Someone came out of the room saying, 'What's that noise? What's that noise?'

We all shrugged. 'We don't know.'

They went back into the room. Oh dear, this is a little bit embarrassing, I thought, as the buzzing continued. It was doing everyone's head in. Ben Stiller must be able to hear this noise. Maybe it's putting him off his stride.

'Alison!' I heard someone yell.

I jumped and the buzzing stopped. 'What?'

The chief PR was coming my way. 'You've been leaning on the doorbell of Mr Stiller's room!' she said sternly.

Everyone in the corridor turned to stare. 'Oh, is it me?' I said, trying to act as if I wasn't too bothered, but secretly I was thinking, Earth, open up and swallow me now!

I had another embarrassing moment the first time I met John Travolta. That day, I had a chauffeur to take me to London in a very nice car that had blacked-out windows and, as we arrived at the hotel with an hour and a half to spare before the interview was due to take place, I decided to do my makeup before I went in.

So far, so good: I was nice and early; I was relaxed; I had time to enjoy myself.

I got out my hand mirror and started doing my face. Now, whenever I do my makeup, I do half my face first, because I like to see the 'before' and the 'after' and how different they are. It's just a silly quirk I have: I'll do my foundation over half of my face and marvel at the difference it makes. It's for my own benefit. I'm entertaining myself. It's a mini-makeover, and I'm doing it to make myself laugh. I just find myself funny – and if you don't find yourself funny, who else will?

The next thing I knew, there was a man standing outside the car, using my blacked-out window as his mirror. He had obviously just been for a run because he was in his tracksuit and looking a little bit sweaty. He was smoothing his hair back and properly checking himself out; he could see himself but he couldn't see that I was inside.

Well, it was only John Travolta. Looking in my car and using my window as a mirror to check himself out! It seemed as if he was looking at me, but he couldn't see me. Meanwhile, I'm on the other side looking him straight in the eye. He had absolutely no idea that The Hammond was behind the window.

'Oh, my God, there's John Travolta, right there,' I screeched at my driver. 'He's looking in the car!'

'Alison, don't say anything,' the driver said.

'I've got to say something! It's John Travolta.'

'Just wait. You're going to be interviewing him in an hour and a half,' he said.

'Yes, but he's right there!'

I rolled down the window. John Travolta and I were now practically face to face. 'John,' I said.

'Yeah,' he said, in his American twang. I think he was a little bit taken aback to see that someone was in the car.

I smiled. 'I'm interviewing you later.'

'Okay,' he said.

There was a bit of a pause and then I added, 'All right then, bye.'

I didn't have anything else to say. I hadn't thought it through.

'Bye,' he said.

He went off and I wound the window back up. When I looked in the mirror to start doing my makeup again, I suddenly remembered that only half of my face was done. Cringe! What must he have thought of me? Who is this crazy woman, this total weirdo, with her face half made up?

I was still buzzing from our encounter when I went into the interview. By then, I had all my makeup on, obviously. 'Have we met before?' he asked, with a puzzled smile.

'Nah,' I replied.

'Are you sure?' he said. 'Like, a few years ago?'

'No, never seen you before,' I lied, and we got on with the interview.

Junkets

What's the secret to delivering a great celebrity interview? Here is my blueprint for doing this job.

The first thing to remember at a film or music junket is that you literally have five minutes with a celebrity. Having so little time to do your interview means that you've got to strike up an instant rapport. You're on show from the second you walk through the door and every moment counts, from start to finish.

I always think there needs to be a beginning, a middle and an end to an interview, just like there is to a movie. So I call my interviews 'mini movies'.

The beginning: when I'm interviewing a celebrity, we'll start by talking about their film or new music, because that's the reason why we're there.

The middle: here we'll maybe get some juicy gossip and you'll see their personality coming out.

The end: the last section usually involves me doing a game, a song, a quiz or an audition with them, to give us all something to smile about.

And finally, the payoff (for me!): the interview should end with a crescendo, something big, something good – like a kiss, a hug or a fist pump.

Another important thing to remember is that, although I'll occasionally connect with a celebrity and we'll genuinely have a lovely time, at the end of the day they're not my mates and we're not going to be hanging out afterwards. We're both there to do a job: they've got to promote whatever they're talking about and I've got to deliver a lovely interview that can be cut, edited and shown on TV. So when I talk about getting cosy with Denzel or Pierce, I'm doing it for the lols.

Ah, but I can still dream, can't I?

Hammond love

I can't think why I enjoy interviewing Hollywood heart-throbs. But for some reason I like sitting opposite fantastically handsome men and having a laugh with them.

So, as you can imagine, I had a great time interviewing Keanu Reeves about his movie *John Wick 2*. After talking about the film's fight scenes in some detail, I was some-how able to move on to the fact that his mum is originally from Essex. Keanu agreed to take part in my Essex-based quiz, but unfortunately, he didn't know what a 'vajazzle' was, and had trouble getting his tongue round 'well jel', the *TOWIE* abbreviation for 'well jealous'. Finally, I gifted him a candle with my face on the side. 'What's the flavour?' he asked.

'Black Cherry,' I said.

I take people as I find them, but when I interviewed Rus-sell Crowe in 2007 for his movie *American Gangster*, I don't think I was expecting him to be the pussycat he turned out to be. I was nervous – I won't lie – and when I went to say, 'Your last film, *A Good Year*, was all about success,' it came out as, 'Your last film, *A Good Year*, was all about sex.'

Cringe! You can see what was on my mind, can't you? Yes! *Gladiator!*

Fortunately Russell laughed and instantly warmed to me. My producer had brought along a guitar, as he'd heard that Russell liked playing, but I left it outside and waited to see how things went first. When he asked me to fetch it, I wondered what would happen – and then Russell Crowe played the guitar and serenaded me. Result! I was his backing singer and although I warbled my part, he didn't seem to care. It was fantastic.

It was also fantastic meeting Denzel Washington in 2007, at the same junket for *American Gangster* where I met Russell Crowe. (I know! Double whammy!) Again, I was incredibly nervous because Denzel is one of my all-time idols, but we instantly got on. When I cut in and interrupted him while he was talking (still nervous!) and then apologized, he said sternly, 'It's all right. Just don't do it again!' and then burst out laughing.

A little later on, he said, 'You remind me of my sister,' and I was a little bit disappointed, but it was better than nothing, I suppose.

Since then, me and Denzel have had a couple of really funny encounters. The last time we met, I started the interview by saying, 'Badass, vigilante, big, Black, beautiful, scary, but that's enough about me, babes . . .'

A few minutes into the interview, we were laughing so much that I threw away my notes and went in for a kiss early.

'Sorry, I've put my lipstick on you,' I said, leaning in to wipe his cheek.

'You. Are. Crazy!' he declared, and we dissolved into giggles again.

I can't count how many celebrities I've kissed, from Will Smith, Pierce Brosnan, Patrick Swayze and Denzel Washington to Hugh Jackman and Leonardo DiCaprio. That's something I've noticed about Hollywood stars: they're all up for a bit of Hammond love.

My kind of man

A couple of years ago, on *This Morning*, I got chatting with Phil and Holly about love and romance.

'What's your type?' Holly asked.

'Someone who makes my heart sing. Someone who makes me laugh,' I said. 'That's pretty much what we all want, isn't it, guys? I'm not necessarily drawn to people in the same industry as me. I don't care what job a man has, as long as he's driven in his work and he's got a little something about him. Someone kind,' I continued, 'who can tell me about myself and say, "Shut up now, Alison, you're embarrassing yourself." Someone who can control me a little bit.'

'What *don't* you want?' Phil asked.

'I don't want someone too controlling!' I said quickly, which sounds a bit like a contradiction.

To be honest with you, I want someone who just gets my lifestyle. A man who knows that if I don't call or text, it's because I'm busy. It's not because I'm with anybody else or I don't love him any more.

So, I'd like someone who is secure in himself, who can see me flirting with The Rock and be okay about it, because he knows I'm coming home to him at night.

Wait a second, did someone mention The Rock?

Now there's a man my mum didn't purse her lips at.

Did I forget to mention that almost no one was good enough for me, in my mum's eyes? Or that, when I introduced her to the men in my life, she'd make it plain if she wasn't keen – she'd purse her lips and in that moment we all knew they weren't going to become part of the family? But Mum absolutely loved the thought of me and The Rock actually being together. I think, in her head, we *were* together. She'd never met him, but with my mum it was all about the look – and, trust me, The Rock had the look. He was the man she wanted her daughter to be with. 'You look so good together!' she'd say.

I met The Rock, the wrestler-turned-actor and producer from the *Fast & Furious* movies, in March 2017.

'We've never met? Wow, after all these years,' he said, at the start of the interview.

I couldn't stop smiling. 'Babes, I have been waiting for this moment.' I looked down at my body. 'As you can see, I've got the rolls, you've got The Rock. Let's rock and roll, baby!'

He roared with laughter. 'Come on, baby!'

And off we went.

We raced through our chat about his upcoming *Baywatch* film with Zac Efron: I showed him the lifeguard swimming costume I was wearing under my top; he showed me what his pecs look like when he flexes them in slow motion.

I know – oh, my gosh! He can raise one eyebrow as well.

I moved on to asking him whether he was serious about considering a presidential bid in 2020, something that had been widely reported at the time.

'Is it true, first of all?' I asked.

Just imagine it. President Rock of the USA!

'It's true that I would consider it,' he admitted, and went on to say how flattered he was that it had blown up in the media.

'You'd win,' I interrupted. 'You'd basically win, babes.'

He smiled. 'I mean, I—'

'You need to do it,' I said, then burst out, 'You need a first lady!'

He grinned. 'That's me and you,' he said.

Yes!

The next thing I knew, The Rock was pretending to propose to me.

'Rock, what you doing, babes?' I asked. 'You're on one knee.'

'Uh, I'm asking, will you marry me?' he said.

I stifled a sob. 'Are you serious?'

'Yeah,' he said. 'I've wanted this since the moment we met!' I snatched the ring from him. 'Does it fit? I love you so much!'

'I love you too.'

We exchanged kisses. 'We're getting married!' we yelled.

'I'm so happy we did this,' he said. 'The pre-nup is coming,' he added, under his breath. 'It's the size of an encyclopedia.'

I left our meeting in fits of laughter, but even better was to come when we met again that December. Kevin Hart and The Rock were in London to promote their movie, *Jumanji: The Next Level*, and we had a great chat about filming in the jungle and Kevin and Dwayne's 'bromance' – sorry, 'dudeship'.

'Obviously, the last time I saw you, two hundred and seven days ago, we got engaged,' I said to The Rock, finally.

'We got engaged,' he said, nodding.

'My lawyers got in touch with your lawyers . . .' I went on.

'They did.' He exchanged a look with Kevin.

'The pre-nup's sorted,' I added.

I'd worn a flowing white dress to the interview, but with a lovely lime green tabard over the top to hide it. 'So I was thinking,' I said, 'why don't we just get married today?'

The Rock laughed.

'I'm so glad you're here, Kevin, because I went online and ordained you as a minister,' I went on, pulling out a bona fide minister's certificate.

'Woah, this is happening right now,' Kevin said delightedly.

Before he had time to think, I had my veil on, I had my flowers; I'd taken off the lime green tabard. We gave a script to Kevin. My producer pressed play on the music box: wedding music started up and confetti came down from the ceiling. We even had a cake. The Rock was getting married to me!

It was one of the funniest interviews ever.

Two years later, just after he married his long-term girlfriend, Lauren Hashian, another journalist from *This Morning* interviewed The Rock on the red carpet and asked him whether he had anything to say to me.

'Alison, I'm sorry. I got married,' he said, looking into the camera.

Emily Blunt was standing next to him at the time. 'He's serving you the papers,' she chipped in.

'Yes, I am serving you the papers – now – but I'll call you tonight,' he said, with a cheeky wink.

Ruined! We made a big thing on *This Morning* of how The Rock had dumped me. They filmed me sobbing under a blanket in the dressing room because I was so upset he'd married someone else. It was silly, but we had a good laugh doing it.

I've still got The Rock's picture up in my kitchen and it makes me smile every time I look at it.

Dreamboats

The Rock is the only celebrity I've 'married' during an interview, but I've flirted with quite a few others. Michael Bublé is one of my favourites. The first time I interviewed Michael, in 2008, I rated him as my most fun person to interview. But before long Hugh Jackman had stolen that title because I didn't see Michael for another whole decade – and, yes, I am that fickle.

When I told Michael that Hugh was my new number one, he was not happy. 'Do you know how many times in the last ten years I've thought about you?' he said.

I was wearing a Christmas top with a photo of the two of us emblazoned over it. But he topped my top by getting out some of the notes he claimed he'd written me over the years: 'I love you'; 'Miss you'; 'Thinking of you.' (All written in the same marker pen – fishy, or what?)

It was such fun – there was no stopping us and the innuendoes were flying. I got out some mistletoe. We kissed. We agreed to kiss on cheeks but I turned my head at the last minute and went for the mouth! We were both really tickled by that. I honestly found it very difficult to control my laughter.

The last time I saw Michael Bublé, he said, 'I'm not

kissing you today, because it gets me into trouble with my wife.'

Ruined!

As for Hugh Jackman, I've met Hugh three or four times now and each time it's just a pleasure. 'It never feels like an interview with you,' he says, and I feel the same.

If we're playing a game, he's all for it; if we're singing, he's totally into it. And when I met him in 2017, we had an absolute ball in the hotel room where the interview took place.

'Hugh, can I just say, we've met so many times and I feel like there's a lot of chemistry between us,' I said, at the start of the interview.

'I *know* there's a lot of chemistry between us,' he agreed.

'You know it, I know it . . .'

'Everyone feels it,' he went on. 'People are uncomfortable in the room. It's a should-we-be-here kind of feeling.'

'So I'm going to call this what it is,' I said. 'It's not an interview.'

'Right, what is it?' he asked, looking ever-so-slightly confused.

I turned to the table beside us and pulled off a cloth to reveal champagne and chocolates. 'It's a date!' I declared.

'Yeah, baby!' He laughed. 'It's a date.'

We drank champagne; he fed me chocolates; I fed him chocolates. We talked a little bit about his latest *Wolverine* film. It was heaven. The funniest moment of the interview was when he started feeding me olives on a cocktail stick. I was really enjoying them and then the cocktail stick got stuck; he couldn't get it out because it was wedged between my gappy teeth. It was a little bit awkward but also quite funny.

Now, although you see me flirting with all these celebrities – Michael Bublé, Hugh Jackman, The Rock – at the end of the day, guys, it's just acting. It's not real. They're all married. But for those five minutes that I'm interviewing these A-list celebrities, they have the opportunity to pretend that I am their wife. And they really seem to enjoy it.

Result!

Expectations

There are so many rumours and opinions flying around in this industry that you can't listen to what people say. Take Harrison Ford, for instance. When I heard I'd been asked to interview him about his movie *Blade Runner 2049*, I was warned that he's not a huge fan of being interviewed.

I met Harrison and Ryan Gosling, the other star of *Blade Runner 49*, in a hotel in London. I had my questions ready; I was ready, I thought.

Only I wasn't ready for what came next.

When Harrison and Ryan arrived, I pointed out some whisky glasses that me and my producer had placed on a small table by the window. 'I got these glasses in because they're from the original *Blade Runner*.'

'Oh, cool,' Ryan said.

'I thought, attention to detail. The fans will probably like that.'

He picked up the glass. 'That's so cool you did that.' He put it down. 'Are you a fan of the original?'

'Never seen it,' I said, and started laughing.

It was a genuine belly laugh, a laugh that tells you I can't believe how honest I've just been. It's a cross between 'I can't believe I've just said that!', 'Oh, my God, what am I like?' and 'Ah. I just want to die.'

Ryan clapped and laughed. Harrison stirred and smiled. 'I appreciate your candour,' Ryan said.

The interview began. I had broken the ice but was still really nervous knowing that I had to speak to Harrison. The. Big. Star.

'Bleak, dystopian, an absolute nightmare, to be honest with you. That's just my interviewing technique,' I said. 'Let's talk about the movie, *Blade Runner 2049*.'

Harrison started smiling. 'Cheer up,' he said.

'Well, you know, it's a bit of a bleak day.' I pointed to the grey sky outside.

'No, it's not. It's a lovely day in London and let's keep it that way. This is not the introduction we were promised. Bring me on with a little happier music, you know.'

Ryan was creasing up in his chair. Somehow I'd managed to turn the tables around.

I started asking another question. Ryan poured out some whisky. 'You having a drink?' I said, interrupting myself.

'I feel that's where this is headed,' he said.

Now Harrison was laughing!

I tried another question. 'Harrison, when you got that call to say, "Listen, we're making another *Blade Runner* and we want you to be in it", what was your reaction?'

'So what?' he said.

Now I was pouring myself a drink.

'Help yourselves. I notice there's nothing left for me,' Harrison said grumpily.

Even though I don't drink, I sipped my whisky. 'I needed that. I've warmed up,' I said.

Unexpectedly, Harrison started laughing again. Ryan exhaled loudly and Harrison went back to my question. 'They said, "Would you be interested?" And I said . . .' He paused.

'How much?' I butted in.

'Show me the money!' He laughed. By now, I was literally crying my eyes out, it was so funny. He reached for Ryan's whisky.

We were all at it!

We barely got through any more questions. I asked about Ryan's jumper, because apparently he's really into knitting. That made him laugh. Harrison was chuckling away and we descended into this cacophony of us all just having a massive laugh, as you'll see if you watch it online. I was genuinely laughing from the gut and you only see me laugh like that when I'm at my most relaxed. When you hear that nasty laugh – which I can't stand, because it's so loud sometimes – you'll know. It's like my meditation laugh, when I'm feeling comfortable, which is such a nice feeling.

We had four minutes together, and by the end of it I thought, That was fun, but I've not even got an interview here. There is nothing about the film. All we've done is drink whisky, talk about glasses and money, and laugh.

But the interview went down really well when it went out on *This Morning*. A few days later, a friend phoned and said, 'Have you seen what's happened online?'

'No?'

'Everyone has picked up on the fact that Harrison Ford

never even smiles in interviews but is laughing his head off with you.'

Suddenly, it was in every magazine in America. It was in all the New York papers and went all the way to Australia. It made all the US TV programmes. Wendy Williams was even talking about it on her talk show. It was just mad. A million people watched it online, then two million and three million and ten million. It shot off the planet.

Oh, my God, I thought. It's the worst interview I've ever done.

People were saying I was a good interviewer, but I was dying at how bad that interview was. If you were a movie-goer, you would have got absolutely nothing from it and I looked like an idiot because I hadn't watched the original *Blade Runner.*

Look how many other interviews I've done, I thought. Some of them are so good, and the only interview that blew up was that one.

I've been doing celebrity interviews since 2003, but back then, social media didn't exist. Otherwise, the fun I had with Pierce Brosnan would probably have gone viral; me dancing for Britney Spears would have gone viral. My Donny Osmond interview is hilarious, but it's not even online. All of these interviews took place at a time when it wasn't about social media. It was just about watching it on *This Morning* and you had to be there to see it, or miss it.

I'd love to meet Harrison Ford again. I've only inter-viewed him once and I thought he was amazing. So you can't listen to other people: you've literally got to take these celebrities as you find them.

If you find them to be not very nice, well, that's your impression. You have to remember that we're all human and we're going to have off-days; we're not always going to be nice and that's okay. It's okay to have moments when you're not yourself. If someone isn't very pleasant for ten seconds, or even a minute, it doesn't define who they are for the rest of their life. It is what it is – they've had that moment when they haven't been very pleasant, and we need to have space to make mistakes in life. We need to make space for our mistakes. Sometimes we mess up, but we can't have that held against us for the rest of our lives. And in the world of social media, I really feel that that's what happens. But we can learn from messing up. We can make those mistakes and be a better person.

There have been times in my life when I've messed up and might not have come across very nicely to someone – I'm only human, at the end of the day – but that doesn't define who I am as a person. I can learn from it and move on; I can apologize and say sorry. In this cancel-culture society, we need to make space for mistakes and not be so judgemental and condescending to people, or write them off. We shouldn't be so ready to cancel somebody out for saying or doing something we perceive as wrong. It's okay to say or do the wrong thing because we're all learning and growing. I want my kid to have the space to make mistakes as he's growing up in this world, not to worry about what he's going to say or do. I want my son to be free to speak his truth without fear of being cancelled. That's my wish for Aidan.

Since the pandemic started, I've been doing my celebrity interviews over Zoom. It's quite bizarre, because it's genuinely like having Julie Andrews, James Corden or John Legend over for tea. It's a lot more personal than seeing them at a junket – it's ten times more personal – because they're in my kitchen, having a full-on Zoom chat, the sort of thing you'd only usually do with your friends and family.

I like it: the whole lockdown has made people less starry; they're a lot more normal, because they realize we're all exactly the same. We've been through something together, including the celebrities. We all know what it's like to go through a pandemic: to be fearful and be locked down. This is something that transcends celebrity.

One of my main questions is: 'How's lockdown been for you?'

Their answers show their vulnerable side and you see we're all exactly the same and there's no such thing as celebrity, really. Yes, we celebrate some of the amazing things they've done, but they're just normal people, like us. They've all been scared; they've all been locked down with their kids and had to go through home schooling, which is exactly what we've been through. It's nice, that moment of realizing that these people are just people. We're all just people.

7. A WHOLE NEW WORLD

I was never really one for making plans, except when I absolutely had to. I tended to travel from one moment to the next, taking what enjoyment I could along the way – and I'm still the same.

This often meant that life happened to me, rather than me thinking, Right, I'm going to do this and then I'm going to do that. And never was this more apparent than when it came to love and becoming a mum, which all came as a bit of a surprise, if I'm honest . . .

Nourddine

Now that I was a regular on *This Morning*, I'd started getting a few other little jobs here and there. I'd been a guest panellist on *Loose Women* and appeared in a couple of episodes of *Doctors*, and in 2003 I was a regular guest on ITV's *Turn on Terry* with Terry Christian, a late-night chat show about television. *Turn on Terry* was a brilliant job, because I got to comment on TV programmes and spend time with Terry Christian, who is just so intelligent and interesting. I really looked up to him and was flattered that he wanted me on his show. It was nice to get out of Birmingham and go to Manchester for a change. The vibe in Manchester is completely different and I really like the Mancunian accent. We filmed in a warehouse in the town centre, so we were right in the heart of things. It was exciting to rock up there every week to do this cool underground programme in front of a live studio audience.

There were always seats to fill in the studio, so one week I texted my friend Jack, who lived in Manchester, and asked him along. I knew Jack from Tunisia, where he'd been one of the reps at the resort. 'Bring a friend,' I told him. 'The more the merrier!'

Jack texted back and said he would come with his flatmate.

On the night, Jack and his mate were running late and just before we were about to start filming, my phone rang. 'Are we in time? We're here, we're here!' Jack said, sounding flustered.

I ran outside to meet them and that was when I saw Nourddine for the first time, sitting in Jack's car. Jack's mate had curly brown hair and soft brown eyes that sparkled with humour. We smiled at each other and his smile radiated so much warmth that I felt myself light up inside. I was completely taken aback. It was an instant connection.

Wow, he's lovely! I thought. I couldn't wait for him to come into the studio.

After the show, Nourddine invited me and Jack to go for a meal at the Italian restaurant where he worked, in the Trafford Centre. As the evening wore on, I found myself really enjoying his company. There was something about Nourddine that drew you in, a certain *je ne sais quoi*. He was charismatic, he was calm and chilled out, and seemed quite sure of who he was. There was even a hint of arrogance that reminded me of my dad.

I was partial to a Tunisian man and everything about Nourddine said Tunisia to me, which was nice because it was ages since I'd been there. Tunisia connected us, and when I started speaking Arabic to him, he was blown away. It was surreal for me to find myself speaking Arabic in England, and I liked it.

'Do you want to meet up again next week, when you're back in Manchester?' Jack suggested.

'We won't come and watch the show,' Nourddine added

(obviously bored by the show already!). 'Just come over to our flat and I'll make some couscous for you,' he said.

'Yeah, I'm up for that!'

Nourddine and I swapped numbers and spent that week texting each other. I couldn't wait to see him again. Something was telling me that he was The One and what was brilliant was that he was Jack's friend and came with a seal of approval.

The couscous was lovely, and so was Nourddine. He made me laugh so much. He made me laugh from the belly and even now, when I'm around him, you'll hear my big laugh all the time.

Before long, we started going out together. I wasn't fully over my relationship with Ben, so maybe at first Nourddine stepped into that gap. I was still in touch with Ben but our lives had gone in different directions: he'd texted me to say he was getting married to a Tunisian woman and I'd texted back to say how pleased I was for him. I really did wish him the best, even though a part of me was still in love with him. He was always going to be the one that slipped away.

But if at first I saw Nourddine as a substitute for Ben, things quickly changed, because I soon fell in love with him. He was the opposite to Ben, as it turned out. Ben was really shy, whereas Nourddine was more outgoing. I liked the way he made me feel. He was a nice guy, very caring, always looking out for me; he had a really affectionate nature. He was interested in other people and absorbed information like a sponge.

I've had relationships with people who have struggled with never being acknowledged when they're out and about with me. They find it rude when people focus only on me. But Nourddine was fine about it. He got it and because he's a people guy, he was comfortable chatting to strangers. 'Give me your camera and I'll take a picture,' he'd offer, when people stopped us to talk to me. Or he'd step back and let us get on with it.

He had the same zest for travelling that I did, so we went to Jamaica together, we went to America. We went to Disneyland, Paris.

I'd say, 'Shall we go away this weekend?'

His face would light up. 'Yeah, all right! Where shall we go?'

'Let's go to Madrid.'

'Yeah!'

He was always up for getting on a plane.

My mum came on a couple of holidays with us and she and Nourddine got on well. Mum was the sort of person who needed you to give her a bit of love and Nourddine did all the right things: he gave her flowers and brought gifts to the house whenever he came for a meal. He always called her Mrs Foster and she was happy with that; she didn't correct him.

In February 2004, I went to LA for a shoot with *This Morning*. It was all about the Oscars and the films and actors that had been nominated.

Nourddine stayed in England, but we were on the phone to each other every day. On Valentine's Day, he phoned and said, 'Have you got the flowers I sent you?'

'Have you sent me some flowers?' I said excitedly. 'That's so nice, but I haven't got them.'

'What? They should have sent them up,' he said. 'Can you go down to Reception and see if they're there? I won't be happy if they haven't arrived.'

'All right, then. I'll go now.'

Off I went down to Reception – to find Nourddine standing at the desk with a bunch of flowers! On Valentine's Day in Los Angeles, when I thought I'd left him at home.

'What are you doing here?' I screeched.

Since I genuinely thought I would just be collecting some flowers, I couldn't have been more surprised.

His face broke into a grin. 'I thought I'd come and visit, babes.'

My heart just melted. It was the nicest thing anyone had ever done for me.

'Babes! This is amazing!' I said, feeling overwhelmed. Tears welled in my eyes. 'This is the best day of my life.'

I was so excited, so happy, and even though I was working, we managed to have a brilliant few days together in LA.

The test

Life was fun and romantic with Nourddine, but when I found out I was pregnant, I wasn't sure how he was going to feel about becoming a dad. We had only been together for a year: we had never talked about marriage or babies and we lived in different cities – he was in Manchester and I was in Birmingham.

To be honest, I don't think I was really the sort of person who was suited to having a child. I was travelling around the world doing this fantastic job that I loved. My life was all about me and I was a bit selfish.

I had never been broody. I had never thought, Yes, I'd like to have a baby.

And yet the moment I discovered I was pregnant everything changed. Straight away I felt connected. Straight away I started thinking, Oh, wow, I have to take care of this baby! And I have to look after myself so that I can take care of my little baby!

It was such a pleasant surprise, and so exciting: I was uplifted. The pregnancy was an accident but I was more than happy to go with the flow. This is my new trajectory, I thought, and I love it!

But I did wonder what Nourddine would say. If

the pregnancy had taken me by surprise, how would he react?

Well, he was as thrilled as I was. 'I've always wanted to be a dad,' he said, his eyes shining. 'This is so exciting!'

His reaction made me so happy. This is going to be amazing, I thought, with relief.

We hugged each other tightly. 'Can you believe this?'

'Let's go out for an Indian tonight, to celebrate,' Nourddine said.

'Okay!'

Before I went to meet him, I popped round to my mum's to tell her the good news. Her reaction was a mix of excitement and horror, because at first I think she was in shock at the realization that her little baby had grown up. I could tell she was thinking, Oh, my God, my Alison! What, she has sex?

'Are you going to get married?' she asked me.

'I don't know. I don't think so.'

'Well, maybe it's something to think about now,' she said, and I could see that she was worried about whether Nourddine was going to stand by me.

That night at the restaurant, we sat at a table in a dim candlelit corner. As we toasted the future, Nourddine took my hand and gave me a rose, which I've still got to this day, pressed, in a book. Then, to my surprise, he pulled out a ring box, opened it and said, 'Will you marry me?'

I was bowled over. 'Yes, I'd love to marry you!' I said. 'But are you only asking me because I'm having a baby?'

He smiled. 'Well, yeah, if you're having my baby I think we should get married.'

'At least you're honest,' I said, laughing. 'Where are we going to stay? Let's get a place together in Birmingham.'

'Or you could move to Manchester and live with me?' he suggested.

'Oh, no, I want to be near my mum.'

It was an instinctive reaction and I was sure he'd understand that you want to be near your mum when you have a new baby, especially if it's your first. That's when you need your nearest and dearest more than ever.

He frowned. 'But I need to be near my sister.' His sister had just found out she was pregnant and he felt a responsibility towards her.

Suddenly we had this whole situation about where we were going to live.

I swallowed hard. 'Babes, I really don't want to be in Manchester.'

'Well, I really don't want to be in Birmingham,' he said, shaking his head sadly.

'We've got an issue then, haven't we? We've got a bit of a problem.'

'Yeah.'

We went to Tunisia to meet his mum, which was fun, but we couldn't resolve our battle over where we were going to live. There was no getting around it: Nourddine's work and family were in Manchester, but I wasn't ready to move away from my mum, especially now that the baby was coming.

Maria, Maria

Mum's life had changed quite a bit since my childhood days. She had taken advantage of the right to buy her council house in Kingstanding and she'd bought it, sold it and moved on to another house. In the mid-nineties, while I was out in the real world trying to find my feet after college, Mum had landed a job at the probation service as an agency secretary. She must have got a taste for law and order while she was working there because she quickly moved on to become a community service officer, driving groups of low-level offenders to fulfil their community service orders by painting a school or a church, or gardening in a park. Mum would supervise her group on the job and take care of them while they worked, overseeing their meals. She had the ability to get on with everyone, so they all absolutely loved her.

Next, she became a bail support officer working at Dudley, Walsall and Solihull courts, where she met Clive, a policeman, and fell in love with him. Mum and Clive got married in March 1998, and because Clive was a train enthusiast, Mum agreed to have the ceremony at the National Rail Museum in York. That's how much my mum loved Clive – and he was totally devoted to her as well.

Mum's next step was to become a probation service officer within the West Midlands Community Section. There was no stopping her. 'You know, I think I could be a probation officer,' she decided, and her work sponsored her to start a degree course in community justice at the University of Birmingham. Bearing in mind that she had left school at fifteen, this was ambitious. But that was Maria: she was one of those people who, once she put her mind to something, went ahead and did it. She passed her degree and became a probation officer. She smashed it.

At the same time, my sister Saundra was also doing a degree in community justice at the same university, and my nephew, Saundra's son, Matthew, was studying medicine. It was unbelievable. There were three generations of the same family at the same university at the same time. They all did really well and graduated together. They even made the university paper, under the headline: 'The Three Degrees'. I've never been so proud in my life.

Once Mum had got over her surprise that I was pregnant, she said, 'You're twenty-nine. It's the perfect age to have kids.' She was excited more than anything and really supportive. I think she was in awe of me that I carried on working and kept going, but also protective: she came to all my scans and antenatal appointments, which was lovely.

I actually found out I was having a boy live on *This Morning* when I did a scan on the show to find out the sex of my baby. I was a bit embarrassed that I was getting my big stomach out on national TV but it was a lovely feeling when I found out he was a boy. It didn't matter to me what sex the baby was – I just wanted a healthy baby – but I know his dad was buzzing that his first child was going to be a son.

I suppose people were quite interested in Aidan after that, because they'd watched him from the very beginning. Some people even get a bit star-struck when they see him out and about with me. They're interested to see how he's grown. 'I saw you when you was in your mummy's tummy!' they tell him.

He gets a bit embarrassed, but I think he loves it really.

Aidan

I had the perfect pregnancy, as it happens. I felt so good about my pregnant body that I was still at *This Morning* on the sofa chatting and saying my goodbyes two weeks past my due date. I was so overdue that they had to hire a midwife to be with me that day, just in case I suddenly started giving birth on the studio floor. It was very caring of them, but they needn't have bothered. This child was so happy and contented that he did not want to come out of me.

He was properly comfortable. He had lovely food and lovely drink; he had me talking to him, laughing, joking, playing music, going to Zumba classes and dancing. He was having such a nice time and experiencing such a wonderful sense of comfort that he could have chilled in there until he was four years old. There was just no incentive for him to come out and be in the world.

I pretty much went straight from *This Morning* to the Birmingham Women's Hospital that day, because you have to be admitted when you get to two weeks over your due date. I had a lovely time at the hospital. Everyone there was so kind. I don't know if it was because I was off the telly, but they gave me my own room and I felt very special. The only thing that worried me was that, with me being quite a big girl, they said I might need special care when the baby was born. It's a horrible word, but there you are: I was deemed to be an 'obese' mum.

Two days went by, three days, and this baby did not want to come out. I had pessaries, I had the injection to try to start me off. Nothing worked. On 4 February, the day before my birthday, the doctors decided that the baby would have to be born by C-section.

A surgeon came along to my room and said, 'Listen, we're going to take this baby out today.'

'It's my birthday tomorrow; can we wait another day?' I asked.

He shook his head. 'It's not a good idea to wait any longer. And, to be completely honest with you, I'm taking my son to play football tomorrow.'

'Oh,' I said, giving him 'the Ali eyes'. 'Please?'

There was a long pause and then he smiled. 'All right, I'll rearrange my son's football so that I can come in tomorrow and deliver your baby.'

'Thank you so much, Doctor, thank you!' I said.

Yesss! My child was going to be born on my thirtieth birthday, 5 February 2005. I rang Nourddine and gave him the good news. 'Make sure you get here on time,' I said.

'I can't wait!' he whooped.

But I was surprised to see that when Nourddine came to the hospital the next day, he arrived empty-handed. I just couldn't believe he'd rocked up with no flowers, no chocolates, no nothing. It was really unlike him – he was usually so good that way. 'Have you not got me a birthday card or anything?' I asked, wondering if he had something hidden in his jacket.

He gave me a sheepish grin. 'Your birthday present's on its way, isn't it?'

'What do you mean?'

'The baby's your birthday present.'

I realized later that he was too focused on the baby coming to think about anything else, but at the time I felt really upset. 'Er, no, you should really think about getting me a bunch of flowers or something . . .' I said.

I think my pregnancy hormones must have kicked into overdrive, because I was fuming inside, absolutely raging. I can't believe I'm having a child with this man! I thought. He hasn't even bought me a bunch of flowers or a card or some chocolates. What am I doing?

I was upset. He was upset. He said, 'I'll go out and get you something.'

I felt calmer once he'd gone. I reminded myself of all the good times I'd had with him. I thought back to one particular day, a few weeks earlier, when we were on our way into Asda and I'd said to Nourddine, 'Listen, I'm not messing around. I've got a weak bladder because I'm pregnant, so don't make me laugh while we're in here because I'll wet myself.'

Lo and behold, we started giggling about something, I wet myself and left a trail behind in Asda. It was awful. I was so embarrassed about it. 'I told you not to make me laugh,' I said crossly. Then I started laughing all over again.

I was still smiling at the memory when the surgeon came to see me. 'Are you ready?' he said, rubbing his hands together. 'We're going to take you down now.'

'No, you can't! Nourddine's not here!' I yelped.

'I'm sorry,' he said firmly. 'It's time to have your baby now. We can't miss this slot.'

'Please, we've got to wait for Nourddine,' I begged. Oh, my God, look at this, I thought. The dad's gone off to buy me a present and now I'm going to have this child all on my own!

I couldn't believe I'd let Nourddine go. I started having an absolute panic attack.

Luckily, my mum was there, my constant, core support, the angel on my shoulder, always ready with words of reassurance. 'Don't worry, I'll be beside you if he doesn't come,' she said.

She got all scrubbed up and put her gown on, just in case he didn't make it back. As we were on our way to theatre, I spotted Nourddine running round the corner clutching a plastic-wrapped bouquet of ugly petrol-station flowers. 'Come on, come on!' I said.

'Happy birthday,' he burst out, gasping for breath as he held out the flowers to me.

'Thank you!' I laughed, feeling much more like myself now. 'Get scrubbed up. We're going to have a baby.'

In the theatre, I was given an epidural injection in my spine, which felt very weird. As soon as it went in, I felt as though there was fire shooting through my legs and up my body, and then, all of a sudden, I couldn't feel my legs. I had absolutely no sensation at all as I was moved from my trolley bed to the operating table. It was as if I was floating, like an angel, across the room.

Once I was on the operating table, they put some music

on, really beautiful music. I was awake, but there was a divider curtain blocking my view of my body from the waist down. I couldn't see what the surgeon was doing and I couldn't feel a thing.

'A Whole New World' came on the music player, and just at that very moment, a cute, funny-looking baby appeared above the dividing curtain and peeped at me.

I burst out laughing. Oh, my God, I can't believe it! I thought. Is that what I've created?

Covered in gunk and dazed by the new world he had just entered, my floppy little baby didn't exactly look the best. I was in hysterics. 'Aw, he's so cute,' I said. I just couldn't stop laughing.

My mum helped the nurse clean him up and get him ready, and she was the first person to wrap him in a blanket. I was so excited when I heard him cry and knew everything was fine. It's hard to explain the feeling of happiness I felt in that moment, because it was mixed with my relief that the birth had gone well and I hadn't needed special care.

My son, Aidan Hammond, had been born to the Disney track 'A Whole New World'! It was perfect.

Moments later, I had this lovely bundle of fun in my arms and it was the best thing that's ever happened to me. Having a child has enriched my life more than I can say. I was literally besotted with my baby, to the point at which I stopped caring that Nourddine hadn't brought me any flowers and nearly missed the birth. 'Look, Nourddine, he's got your nose!' I said.

'And your eyes,' he said, looking on in wonder.

I was over the moon. It had been a lovely, easy birth and I had the cutest little baby in the world. I couldn't have had a better birthday present. (Not that I would have admitted it to Nourddine, obvs.)

Taxi for one!

Although my love life stretches back more than thirty-five years, it's not a very crowded timeline. My first love was Stephen, one of the kids at school; he was a very good-looking lad and I was absolutely mad about him. We used to walk home from school the same way and if I didn't see him at the end of the day, I'd be devastated: 'He didn't wait for me!'

I used to wait for him, but pretend I wasn't waiting: 'Oh, hi, Stephen,' I'd say, kicking a stone and looking off into the distance.

Then I'd fall into step beside him. Oh, but that walk home never seemed long enough.

I learnt Stephen's phone number off by heart and used to ring him just to hear him saying, 'Hello? Hello?'

I'd listen to him breathe and quickly put the phone down.

It's so embarrassing to remember it now. He's going to read this book and think, What an absolute plonker! I wonder if he had any idea at the time how obsessed I was.

So, Stephen was my first love – and quickly recapping the Hammond world of romance before I roll out the next episode – I had my first kiss with Caleb when I was fourteen. Then I met Hugo and lost my virginity at twenty-one. After that, there wasn't anyone memorable until I worked in Tunisia and went out with Ramsey, the terrible DJ, a couple of holiday reps, and Ben, the one who got away. Then came Nourddine, who moved into a lovely little one-bedroom flat with me a few weeks before Aidan was born and got a job in an Italian restaurant in Birmingham. He still had his place in Manchester, though, and was constantly going back there to see his sister, so it felt as if he was living with me but not living with me. I tried to make the best of it, but it wasn't really working.

I started feeling lonely in the flat when Nourddine was away: it was just me and the baby. But when he came back, I was too preoccupied with Aidan to give Nourddine the attention he wanted. There's so much to do when you've got a newborn baby, what with nappies and bottles and everything, and it's a steep learning curve.

Nourddine was a lovely dad – I can't fault him in that regard – but he didn't know how to be there for me. I felt he wasn't putting enough effort in with me – I didn't feel supported – and over time we realized we weren't compatible. He wanted to be in Manchester and I wanted to be in Birmingham.

I was up and running at work again, out there doing my thing. Two weeks after Aidan was born, I expressed some milk, left Aidan with my mum and went out for the afternoon to interview Will Smith for *This Morning*. A couple of months later, I went to Iceland for a competitions special and Aidan stayed with his dad for four days, so they had a bit of bonding time. But when I came back from

Iceland, Nourddine left for Manchester, and I was alone in the flat again.

You know what? Let's leave it, I thought. This isn't going to work.

On reflection, maybe I was a little bit too quick to quit our relationship, but I had everything I needed – I had my beautiful child – and Nourddine was no longer a priority. I decided there was only one place I wanted to be and that was back in the bosom of my mum. 'Is it all right if I move back home?' I asked her.

Mum was overjoyed. 'Yes, come back!' she said. 'Your room's exactly the same. All your stuff is still here.'

Mum hadn't touched my room because she probably knew deep down in her heart that I was going to come back.

I felt so safe at my mum's. My work was getting busier and busier and it was just easier to have Aidan there with my mum and stepdad. Mum was over the moon to have her baby grandson living with her so it was the best thing I could have done: she and Clive absolutely doted on Aidan, almost as much as I did.

In those early days, Aidan was waking up every two hours and I was barely getting any sleep. I wasn't one to leave him crying: I wanted my baby to be happy, so of course I was going to pick him up when he needed comforting. I wouldn't have done it any other way – and it's not like I've produced someone who clings to his mum all the time. He doesn't want to be around me now: I've grown a kid who does his own thing.

Those interrupted nights took it out of me, though.

Mum could see I was dying of exhaustion, so every now and then she'd have him in her room for a couple of nights so that I could catch up. She was amazing. She helped me with his feeds and nappies. I don't know what I would have done without her. She scooped me up.

Nourddine came to visit most weekends, but Mum insisted that he slept in a different room from me because we weren't married. She was very traditional in that way. We thought it was hilarious: even though we'd had a baby together, he had to sleep in a separate room.

I took to motherhood naturally and easily. As Aidan grew, he chilled out and I had this gift of knowing what he wanted and needed. I could look at him and say, 'He wants something to eat,' or 'He wants to play. He wants to go outside.' It was rare that he'd be crying and I wouldn't know why. It used to surprise my mum how connected we were.

When you have a child, you suddenly understand why you're here on this earth. 'Ah, I get it now,' I kept saying. It's not about you any more: it's about them.

As for me and Nourddine, we were slowly growing apart. We were living in different cities and the distance between us was a major problem – out of sight, out of mind, as they say. We both got on with our separate lives and the gaps between seeing each other grew longer. It happened so gradually that it seemed like a natural progression.

I look back and think that, although we were meant to meet and have Aidan – and I truly believe it was written in the stars – we weren't destined to stay together. Perhaps I should have thought about moving to Manchester but I just didn't see my life there, not while my mum was in Birmingham, and Nourddine clearly didn't want to live in Birmingham. I sometimes wonder whether I would have had more kids if I'd stayed with him, because I do wish I'd had another child. But I have to accept that it wasn't meant to be.

Nourddine and I never did get married and I was as much to blame as he was. I'm not really the best girlfriend because I put my job before relationships. I'm trying to change that and make relationships more of a priority, but it's hard when you've got a job like mine. One minute I'll be at home and the next my work will be phoning me to say, 'You're booked on a flight to New York this evening.'

If you're going out with me, you need to be quite secure in yourself and cool with the idea of me jetting off somewhere at a moment's notice. I'm not going to be around all the time.

Eventually we split up. Nourddine became an every-other-weekend dad, and in time, we saw him as and when he wanted to see Aidan. I used to encourage him to try to be in Aidan's life as much as possible, but it was difficult after he became a taxi driver in Manchester and started working really long hours.

It's weird, because the love doesn't stop, it just changes. It's a different love. It's more respectful. There's a beautiful passage in the Bible that describes love in its ideal form, but I can't remember it very well, so I'm going to have to look it up . . . Here it is, 1 Corinthians 13, and it goes:

Love is patient and kind; love does not envy or boast; it is not arrogant or rude. It does not insist on its own way; it is not irritable or resentful; it does not rejoice at wrongdoing, but rejoices with the truth. Love bears all things, believes all things, hopes all things, endures all things . . .

Basically, love will get you through anything.

Fortunately, Nourddine is a lovely guy. We were never horrible to each other and we're still friends now. It's a pity we couldn't stay together but it wasn't our time. That's just life, isn't it? I'm not bitter about it. I'm just happy that he's still in my life and our relationship is wonderful. We went on to have some amazing times even after we split up – we went to Florida together, to Jamaica, to Paris and Sydney. We travelled the world together as a family so that Aidan could have holiday time with his dad because he dotes on his dad. Obviously, he dotes on me more. But he absolutely dotes on his dad.

Nourddine is now married to the loveliest Tunisian woman and they have three children, so Aidan's got a brother and two sisters, and they absolutely love me. They're all under the age of five and they're glued to me whenever they see me – I think it's the big boobs. All we do is cuddle. When we see them it feels like we're one big family and I can't stop myself saying, 'Can't we all just live together? We'll be happy. Come on!'

My brother finds it amazing. 'You're so cool, having Nourddine and his wife and kids over,' he says. 'Doesn't it bother you at all?'

It took us a long time to get to that point, but I find

things are a lot easier when you've got love in your heart – and, ultimately, we all love each other. Aidan loves his dad; his dad loves Aidan; I get on with Nourddine's wife and I love his kids, which is mad, really. So we all get on, just like Bruce Willis and his family.

My one son

Even when he was a baby, Aidan was a lovely person to be around. I just loved his little character. He had a beautiful energy and I always felt as if he knew what was going on. When I got upset that things hadn't worked out with Nourddine, he'd give me a look as if to say, 'Don't worry, everything is going to be all right. It doesn't matter that my dad is not with you any more. We'll be okay, just me and you.'

I often call him 'my one son' – he's my only child, after all. I'm quite a protective mum and even now, if I have to go away for work, my brother will come and stay in the house with Aidan until I get back. It's not that he needs looking after: it's just that I don't feel comfortable leaving him alone quite yet, not until he's eighteen, anyway. I just love him so much!

Aidan is so kind and loving and he's absolutely brilliant in social situations. He's not too in-your-face and he's always looking out for me. He's just a great person to be around, a lovely person. Everyone who meets him says, 'You're so adorable, so nice!'

And it's true – he's got a really nice nature. The only time I've struggled as a parent was during the 2020–21 lockdown, because it was difficult to keep him motivated at school when there was nothing to be motivated about. It wasn't easy to be a parent during lockdown, but that was the only time I found it hard, I think. Basically, I'm happy when Aidan's happy, and he's usually very contented.

He's always been quite independent. He likes to do things off his own bat, which sometimes makes us clash because he can be so stubborn in his thinking. He reminds me of myself, really, but I guess we were born on the same day so there are always going to be similarities in our personalities. We're both Aquarius and we know what we want, so I can't really guide him in his career. He's got his heart set on the direction he wants to go in, and it's definitely towards Formula 1: he loves cars and is off to study motor sports at college. As a parent, all I can be is kind and wise in everything I do, and try to guide him along the correct path.

It used to be trains when he was really young. He used to love trains: looking at trains, going on trains. Whenever he was restless, I'd take him by the hand and we'd walk around the corner from Mum's house to the railway track. I'd sit there reading a book while he watched the trains pass by. 'Mum, another train!' he'd squeal.

'Yes, babes. Whoa!' I'd say, glancing up and smiling. Then it was back to my book.

I'd sit there for an hour or two, just to make him happy, and he was as happy as Larry watching the trains go by. He had a little camera and he'd stand up, take a picture, sit down again and wait for the next train. He used to wave to the driver and sometimes the driver would sound his horn in reply, which would delight him. He got all of this joy without even getting on a train, so you can imagine what he was like when we actually took a train journey. He was in his element. By then my stepdad had taken early retirement from the police force and was working as a train manager, so he used to take Aidan on train rides and to steam train museums. Aidan had a lot of fun with his granddad.

Then, suddenly, in his teenage years, he had a complete one-eighty turn towards karts and everything to do with karting. Now it's Formula 1 and Lewis Hamilton. Aidan is obsessed with Lewis Hamilton. His dream is to meet him, one day – and somehow I'll have to make it happen. So far, I haven't had the chance to interview Lewis, but I'm hoping that, for Aidan's sake, I do get to interview him at some point so that Aidan can meet him. (And also, obviously, because he's the greatest Formula 1 driver ever, a fantastic role model and an all-round hero of the modern world!)

The closest we got to Lewis was in the autumn of 2017, when we went to a party where two friends of mine, Jake Wood and Alison (lovely name), were renewing their wedding vows. I'd got to know Jake while I was doing *Strictly Come Dancing* and he'd invited a lot of that year's contestants to the party, including Frankie Bridge from the Saturdays, Tameka Empson from *EastEnders* and Judy Murray. People were taking their kids and I decided to go with Aidan. It was such a good party: it was festival-themed and they even had festival wristbands.

Early on in the evening, Judy Murray came over and said, 'Aidan, I've got somebody I think you'd like to meet.'

Everyone on *Strictly* had heard about Aidan's obsession with Formula 1, but I was very touched when Judy led us over to where a group of people were standing and introduced Aidan to Anthony Hamilton, Lewis Hamilton's dad. Aidan was completely overwhelmed. I've never seen him show so much passion and emotion in all his life. He burst into tears, which was very unexpected, and once he'd got over the shock, his face lit up in a huge grin. He was so happy and animated to be talking to Anthony Hamilton about racing – and Anthony was absolutely lovely with him.

Anthony gave Aidan a big hug and chatted to him all night long. He gave him lots of advice. 'You should come and drive at the karting track near us and we'll come and watch you,' he said, towards the end of the evening.

'Really?' Aidan said. 'Mum, will you take me? Will you take me?'

'Sorry, I'm busy,' I teased.

A week later, I took my one son to a karting racetrack near Stevenage. 'Will he come, Mum? Do you think he'll come?' he kept asking.

'Well, he might, and he might not. I don't know, darling.'

As promised, God bless him, Anthony and his son, Nick Hamilton, came to the racetrack to watch Aidan race that day. Unfortunately, Aidan wasn't at his best because he was so nervous! But that's all part of the journey of life, isn't it? He'll know to work on his nerves for next time.

It's not always easy being a parent, but I would never, ever discourage anyone from having a child. I would always say, 'You know what? It's going to enrich your life in ways you cannot believe. It's going to be hard. Don't get me wrong, it's not easy, but it will enrich your life.'

On set with Nourddine, madly in love. He was as surprised and thrilled as I was to be having a baby.

With Nourddine and my mum, just before Aidan was born on the best day of my life. Nourddine had finally made it back in time.

Above: My mum, loving life, with her little two-day-old grandson.

Right: On a modelling job for Evans; Aidan was an absolute pro.

My mum, Aidan and his new baby teeth. He was such a lovely baby.

Trying to take a nice family photo in Florida and get Aidan to look at the camera, but he was more interested in his train whistle.

Giving Aidan a little shower at Dunn's River in Jamaica.
It's a bit cold, but he's loving it.

Above: At Disneyland with Jasmine, feeling good.

Right: Me and Elton in action on the red carpet outside his Oscars party. Look how much his husband loves him!

Left: Massage time.

Above: With Oscar-nominated Allison Janney on a night of mistaken identity.

Right: Treated like a Hollywood Star, with all my gift-suite goodies during Oscars week in LA – and yes, this was why I needed to buy a suitcase.

Re-creating an iconic image from the movie *La La Land*, on the spot where it was actually filmed.

Right: My own star on the Hollywood Walk of Fame. It wasn't real, just a sticker, but it managed to last for three days until someone thought, *Who the hell is that?*

Below: When Mum died, some of the producers came to her funeral and presented me with this beautiful photo, which was taken when we went back to my old school for a film for *This Morning*.

And it does. It gives you purpose. It gives you satisfaction. You know where you're heading: you have that goal. My dream, now that Aidan is coming to the end of his school years, is to see him functioning as a normal adult when he grows up. I can't wait to see him earning his own money and doing his own thing, and if he can wash his clothes, tidy his room, iron, cook, clean, look after his personal hygiene and treat women with respect and kindness – in fact, treat everyone with respect and kindness – then I'll have done my job. That's all I wish and hope for, really – to produce a functioning adult who's kind, likeable, independent and can live his own life. Obviously, I'd love him to be around until I'm eighty-five, but it wouldn't be fair on him. I want him to live a full life, enjoy himself and have a family.

I look at Aidan and think: he's bright, he's beautiful, he's charming, genuine, cool, sensitive, kind and funny. He's just lovely and he's got a lovely figure. He is the kid I wanted to be!

Can you tell that I just love everything about my son? I love him and think he's just amazing – and he is amazing. He's got a great life and fantastic friends; he goes to a lovely school and has nice teachers. Everything in his life is good. I mean, look at his mum, for goodness' sake!

What could be better than that, lol?

Jasmine

Aidan was an only child, but he was never lonely growing up. He had lots of friends and was very close to his cousin Jasmine, my sister's daughter. Even though she was a few years older than Aidan, Jasmine was always lovely with him and he really looked up to her. She's the sweetest person – she'd do anything for you. I'm not joking: she's a true angel.

I mentioned earlier that Jasmine was in hospital while I was in the *Big Brother* house. She was diagnosed with Kawasaki's disease when she was three and a half, which meant she had giant aneurysms on both of her coronary arteries. She spent time in hospital on and off after that, bless her, and always had to take medication for her condition. Otherwise, though, she was just a normal kid: she did really well at school and was quite academic; she enjoyed acting and playing the keyboard; she had loads of friends and was a really lovely child.

When Jasmine was twelve, the doctors said she was in heart failure and would need to have a heart transplant later on in life. Then, one Friday, she collapsed at school, out of the blue. Luckily for her, she collapsed into the arms of the only person in the school who was trained in CPR. When he noticed that she didn't have a pulse, his training kicked in and he went straight into life-saving mode.

An ambulance was called and the school phoned my sister Saundra, who rang me to let me know what was happening as she rushed to be with Jasmine. Later, Saundra told me that when she got to the school, she found Jasmine lying on the floor with her clothes cut open and paramedics trying to jumpstart her heart with a defibrillator. Imagine walking into that situation and seeing your daughter sprawled out like that. Nothing could be worse.

Jasmine was taken to Birmingham Children's Hospital, where she had more cardiac arrests. Her condition couldn't have been more serious. 'If she flatlines again, we don't know if we'll be able to bring her back,' the doctors warned Saundra.

They held an emergency meeting and decided it would be best to put Jasmine on an ECMO (extracorporeal membrane oxygenation) machine, which pumps blood outside your body to an artificial lung that adds oxygen and removes carbon dioxide, then pumps the oxygenated blood back into you. They said it would give Jasmine's heart a rest and buy her some time while they looked for a replacement heart. But it involved risk, because the machine had to be connected to Jasmine via tubes in her arteries.

It was up to my sister to make the decision whether or not to take that risk. 'Okay, go ahead,' she said, because there didn't seem to be any other option.

Jasmine was only twelve. We wanted her to live.

Only a day later, on the Saturday, the ECMO machine started to fail. It was catastrophic: Jasmine's body began to swell, and within hours she was so swollen that I couldn't recognize her. I'll never forget seeing the pain and anguish that Saundra and Andy went through during that awful time. We were all beside ourselves with worry.

That night, Saundra went to the hospital chapel and prayed all night long, begging and pleading with God, 'Please don't take my daughter away.'

While Saundra prayed, Matthew, Jasmine's older brother, sat at her bedside round the clock, checking that the nurses were doing what they were supposed to. Luckily for Jasmine, Matthew is a doctor. He wanted his sister's care to be perfect in every way – and it was.

The doctors couldn't move Jasmine so the following day, the Sunday, they sent us all away while they performed a three-hour bedside operation on her to remove blood clots from her chest. The wait was agonizing. I went home to Aidan, feeling absolutely exhausted, and cried my eyes out. They weren't being very positive at the hospital – Jasmine's chances didn't look good at all – and I kept thinking of how I'd been at her birth with Andy, how I'd been the first person to see her head come out and the first to touch her. It was devastating to think we might lose our little angel. It made me appreciate more than ever how precious life is. It made me want to hold my son close to me and never let go.

I felt so nervous about what might happen that I thought I'd better prepare Aidan for the worst. 'We don't know if she's going to make it,' I gently told him, as it was genuinely looking as if Jasmine was going to die. I wanted to be honest with him, but he was so upset I almost wished I hadn't.

That night, my sister phoned me at three in the morning.

'I've just had a call from the hospital,' she said. 'They've got good news and bad news.'

'What's the good news?'

'They've found a heart.'

'You're joking!'

'I'm not – it's on its way to the hospital.'

'What's the bad news?'

'They haven't checked it yet, so they don't know whether we can use it.'

'Oh. Do you want me to come to the hospital?'

'Yes, please.'

I was there within half an hour. My first question when I saw my sister at Jasmine's bedside was 'Is the heart any good?'

At last I saw hope in Saundra's eyes. 'Yes, it is!' she said.

It was the healthy heart of a forty-year-old woman and a perfect match for Jasmine, but there were still reasons to worry. Because she was so ill – the sickest child in the whole of the UK – Jasmine couldn't be moved to Great Ormond Street Hospital in London, where an operation like this would normally be performed. Instead, early the next morning, two heart surgeons from London would be driving up the M1 to Birmingham to perform the first ever heart transplant at Birmingham Children's Hospital.

Please, God, I thought, make sure these surgeons get to Birmingham. Don't let them have an accident on the motorway.

I was incredibly worried that something might happen to them on the journey. I knew how easily car accidents could happen.

The surgeons arrived safely and performed a successful heart transplant, God love them, on the Monday morning, and as soon as Jasmine was stable, a week after having the surgery, she was taken by ambulance to Great Ormond Street Hospital, where she could have the best care possible. She remained there, recovering, for about two months.

Imagine Jasmine: she went to school one day happy and healthy, and the next thing she knew she'd woken up with a new heart. She'd had no preparation, no idea that it was going to happen. And when she woke up they had their work cut out to rehabilitate her, because she had been lying in bed in a coma for weeks and weeks: she couldn't walk; she couldn't even lift her hand.

I'll never forget the day Jasmine left the hospital. We were so happy: my mum was there, the whole family came, and we all wheeled her out together. An image from that incredible day has stayed with me ever since: Jasmine was sitting in her wheelchair, waiting to leave, when suddenly a ray of sunshine streamed through the window above her and lit up her face. Closing her eyes, she put her head back and enjoyed the moment – it was obvious from her expression how special the warmth of the sun felt to her just then. She wasn't thinking about the future or the past, she was simply enjoying being alive. It was beautiful to watch, and I took a picture of her to remember it by.

Jasmine is twenty-three now and one of the most grateful people I've ever come across. She's so thankful in the moment, so happy to be alive. Everybody loves her and she loves everybody. When she comes over to your house, she'll happily sit down and talk to you, and then she'll jump up and say, 'Do you want a drink?' She'll be running around doing things for you in your own house.

Jasmine still has to take medication and go to the hospital to be checked, but she's doing really well in her life. She's amazing: she's got her gold Duke of Edinburgh Award; she's learnt to play piano; she got her teaching degree and now she works as a special-needs teacher. She's absolutely thriving – and she's very much in love, too. At the time of going to press, we're hoping she'll be getting married soon, if we can manage to bring the groom over from Seattle in America, where he's from. So hopefully there will be a groom and there will be a wedding! And guess where it's set to take place? At Birmingham University, where 'The Three Degrees' – Jasmine's granny, mum and brother – studied. Dr Matthew, Jasmine's brother, is giving her away.

Sadly, Jasmine's dad Andy will be missing, though, as he passed away in February 2021, a year and a week after we lost Mum. But, all the same, I know we'll all be so grateful on the day: grateful to the forty-year-old woman who saved my niece's life with her donated heart; and grateful to everyone in the NHS who gave her such good care. What those doctors and nurses did to keep her alive was unbelievable. They all cared so much about Jasmine, which meant a lot to us as we were going through all that crushing worry about her.

As for the NHS – oh, man. Think about what we would have had to do to pay for Jasmine's heart transplant in a country without a free health service: we would probably all have had to sell our houses, and more. An operation like hers must cost the earth! So, when we found out there was a shortage of ECMO machines in the UK, me and Saundra decided to raise £35,000 to buy another: just imagine if there hadn't been an ECMO machine to keep Jasmine alive! She definitely wouldn't be with us today.

Part of the money we raised came from my winnings on a *Who Wants to Be a Millionaire?* special I did alongside John Partridge in 2012: me and John won £50,000, which we shared equally; £25,000 went to his charity, and £25,000 to mine.

And when Jasmine was better, Saundra did a load of fund-raising too so we were able to buy an ECMO machine for the Birmingham Children's Hospital. We were so pleased to be able to give something back. We were so, so grateful for the life of Jasmine.

From Aidan's first scan as a baby to Jasmine's heart transplant – and all the hospital and GP appointments in between – we've got to love the NHS, haven't we? So many of us wouldn't be here without it.

8. BACK TO REALITY

It was the best of times and the worst of times, a tale of two reality shows. Here's what really went on when I did 'the big two', with a spoonful of real reality to finish off!

New home

One of my mum's favourite pastimes was to look around houses that were up for sale. She especially liked viewing show homes that she couldn't afford – and pretending that she could. She loved a show home, and even after she bought one for herself, we went on looking round houses together. I still do it now: I go into houses that I absolutely can't afford and pretend I can. I think, because I'm Alison Hammond off the telly, the estate agents never really question it.

'Yes, yes, this is great, wonderful, love it,' I say. 'I can see this as my room. Aidan, this will be yours . . .'

Sometimes they ask, 'Cash or mortgage?' and I say, 'Yup, cash – cash is in the bank.'

I wish!

I've probably blown my cover now but I don't think I'll ever stop doing it because it's become one of my passions. What can I say? It's something I got from my mum. Me and Mum were constantly on Right Move because on Right Move you can see into people's houses. Maybe I'm just nosy, but I like looking at other people's décor, and so does Aidan. I like to see if people are cluttered or a little bit OCD in their furniture arrangements. And, you never know, one day I will be able to buy the house I really want, with a swimming-pool in the garden.

As my mum used to say, 'You've got to have a dream, Al.'

Me and Aidan had been living with my mum and Clive for about two years when I decided that now would be a good time to get our own place. I had noticed some flats being built two minutes down the road from my mum's so I went to have a look. The flat I viewed was perfect for me: it felt solid and secure and I liked its vibe. It was all about smooth lines and clean surfaces and I'm a big fan of the decluttered style of Mrs Hinch and Stacey Solomon. I also prefer brand new properties, because you don't have to do anything. You just pack your bags and move in.

'Go for it, Al,' my mum said.

So I bought it. Of course, living so close to my mum meant that whenever I needed to go to work, even if it was at a moment's notice, Aidan could just go across the road and stay with her until I came back. Result! Our flat was similar in style to Mum's house and she thoughtfully arranged Aidan's room there to make it exactly the same as his room at home. He had everything in duplicate so that it felt familiar and he would never wake up in the night wondering where he was.

As Aidan grew up and started running around, I began to wish we lived somewhere with a garden. (Human beings are never happy: we always want more!) As well as having space to play, I wanted my son, while he was young, to know how plants grew and where the food on our plates came from. I applied for an allotment and started growing vegetables. I can honestly say that the corn I grew that first year was the most amazing corn you've ever tasted: it just melted in your mouth. I also planted potatoes, carrots and beetroot and they all came up. For a short while, I had the best allotment ever.

The following year, it wasn't as easy to keep it going because I was working quite a lot. I let it go a little bit and it got to the stage where it was getting overgrown.

People started complaining that my little plot was really messy.

'It's not messy, it's *natural*,' I said. 'It's *relaxed*.'

Eventually, it went up before the allotment committee. Do you know what? I thought. Before this gets out of hand I'll just give it back to the council.

I went back to wishing we had our own garden.

A little three-bedroom semi-detached came up for sale around the corner from my flat, about a four-minute walk from my mum's house. It had a lovely little garden and I liked everything about it, especially that it was in a corner, off the beaten track. You wouldn't have known it was there.

Me and my mum went to view it. 'Lovely! Lovely!' Mum cooed, as we looked around. 'The garden is perfect for Aidan. You have to buy it!'

'But I don't think I can afford it,' I said.

'If it's meant to be, something will come along,' Mum said knowingly.

Phone swap

My mum was right. Something did come along. In 2010 *I'm a Celebrity . . . Get Me Out of Here* came along. I hesitated before I agreed to take part in it, though: I really had to weigh it up. On the one hand, I didn't want to spend weeks on end away from Aidan, who was five; on the other, the fee they were offering would really help towards saving for the deposit on my little house and garden. And a part of me was curious about going into the jungle. I'd spoken to people who had done *I'm a Celebrity . . . Get Me Out of Here* and raved about it. Maybe it wasn't as bad as it looked. So I said yes.

Only, when the time came for me to go to Australia, where the show was being filmed, I started to panic. While I was in the jungle I would be completely cut off from the world – and my world was Aidan. I knew he would be fine with my mum – he adored his gran and granddad – but what if he thought I'd abandoned him? What if he needed his mum while I was trapped in the camp? He was still only little, my one son. I felt very protective of him.

'Be practical,' I told myself. 'Aidan will be completely fine.'

At the very least, I wanted to be able to speak to him

right up until I went into the show. I racked my brain for ways to avoid the torture I'd gone through when I was holed up in a hotel without a phone before I went into the *Big Brother* house. How could I get around the chaperone? Bribery? Deceit? Murder?

Just then I had a brainwave, and a few days later, I got on the plane to Australia carrying two phones.

When I met my chaperone out there, she said, 'Can I have your phone, please?'

'Yeah, no problem.' I handed over a dud handset.

'This is the hardest part for some people,' she said, as she put it away.

Instinctively, I patted the pocket where I'd hidden my real phone. 'Yes, I don't know how I'm going to survive without speaking to my family and friends!' I agreed.

That evening in my lockdown hotel room, I used my real phone to ring my mum and speak to Aidan. I know it was a bit cheeky, but sometimes you've just got to do these things.

'Don't get caught using that phone!' my mum said.

'Don't worry, I only use it when I'm on my own in the bedroom,' I assured her. 'How's it all going? I love you and miss you, Mum. How's Aidan?'

'Aidan is fine. He's eaten up all his breakfast and now he's playing with his trains. Here he is now. Oh, my goodness, I can't believe you're going into the jungle! It's so nice to be able to talk to you.'

The show began in mid-November 2010, but I was going in as a surprise late arrival, a few days after the others. Two other campmates, Dom Joly and Jenny Eclair, were going in late before me, and I was slightly nervous that yet another new person coming after them might not be very welcome.

I pictured how the other campmates would react when I arrived out of nowhere. 'She's going to eat all the food and her pants are going to take up the whole washing line!'

'Don't be silly,' I told myself. 'You're over-thinking things. It'll be fine.'

My mum was watching the show back in England, and when I rang her from my hotel room she gave me all the gossip about what was going on in the jungle. 'It's really good,' she said. 'Stacey's done a trial. Dom Joly's just gone in with Jenny Eclair.'

'Really?'

I was only really interested in checking on Aidan to make sure everything was okay with school and his friends. It was as much for me as for him: I needed to have that connection.

Since I was expecting to go through a massive security check before I went into the camp, I turned my phone off as I was leaving the lockdown hotel, put it into the bottom of my suitcase and resigned myself to being out of contact with the world. But because I was a late arrival, nobody went through my bags or pockets so I could have easily taken it with me. Grrr! Knowing me, though, I would probably have dropped it in the creek.

Splash!

Bad times

I arrived in the jungle inside a huge crate covered with chains and padlocks. It had 'DELAYED IN TRANSIT' printed on the side.

Linford Christie and Sheryl Gascoigne were the camp-mates who were sent to find me. 'Hello?' I called, when I heard their voices. I was trapped in total darkness and desperate to get out of the crate.

I think Linford and Sheryl were a bit disappointed when they realized there was a person inside, because they were hoping it would be full of treats. 'Is there anything in there with you?' they asked.

'There's a box of my favourite chocolate,' I said. Terry's Chocolate Orange!

Suddenly, they were interested. 'If you've got goodies in there, we're going to try harder to get you out,' Linford said eagerly.

They were that hungry! It wasn't a good sign and my tummy started rumbling in sympathy.

It took us a while to work out how to unlock the pad-locks on the chains around the crate, but finally I was free. Linford seemed quite pleased to see me. 'I'm glad she's here,' he said later. 'She's funny. She'll crack a few jokes and I think she'll be a real welcome addition to the camp.'

'When we get back, they'll be pleased because we've got chocolate *and* Alison,' Sheryl said.

Wrong!

I was so relieved to get out of that box that I arrived at the camp in high spirits. 'The party's here!' I announced joyfully.

It was the worst thing I could have said. The other campmates turned and stared at me, as if to say, 'Oh, here we go again. Another person.'

Everyone had already bonded and made their friends and I could feel that they didn't want me there. Shaun Ryder wasn't happy at all. As soon as I walked in, he couldn't wait to go. I could have been anybody, I think, and he would have felt the same. Two extra campmates had gone in before me and he didn't want any more arriving.

Straight away I felt the vibe and thought, Maybe I need to tone it down a bit if I'm going to get on with everyone.

I think I did get most people onside after a couple of days, and hopefully they enjoyed me being in there, but I didn't feel comfortable in the camp. Because I hadn't been there all along, I kept thinking I was treading on people's toes. When I was doing the cooking, for instance, people were getting upset because they had their routine already and obviously felt I was disrupting it. It didn't help that hunger was making them edgy and irritable.

The conditions were awful. The camp wasn't nice and clean, like the *Big Brother* house: it was disgusting and uncomfortable. The bed was lumpy. The toilet was rank and absolutely stank. You had to go and wash in the creek, which was freezing cold; you had to wait ages before they delivered your food at night and then you were cooking in the pitch black. It was stressful. It looked a lot easier for the contestants who did the show in 2021 in the Welsh castle, where the toilets were lovely and clean. Even the trials didn't look as hard in 2021. I think I would have loved it in the castle, whereas the jungle was definitely not my cup of tea.

By the second day, I was feeling overwhelmed. Have I made a massive mistake coming here? I wondered.

Every instinct in me was telling me to walk out, but I managed to talk myself out of it.

I was very glad that the lovely Jenny Eclair was in the camp. As one of the two new campmates who'd gone in late before me, she had a good idea of what I was thinking and feeling when I'd arrived. Jenny took me under her wing and showed me a lot of kindness. She could see that I was having a nightmare with the toilet, the washing facilities and my uncomfortable bed, and was really sympathetic. One day she even said, 'You can have my bed tonight,' and went off to sleep in a hammock. How nice was that?

Although I'm resilient, I found it hard to enjoy myself. Every day in that camp felt like a year and I can only shake my head when I hear people saying, 'The jungle was amazing! Absolutely loved it. I found myself and became at one with nature. It really worked out for me.'

Our trials were horrific. I was sent to do the food trial with Jenny and we did our best to support each other, but we were dealing with bugs, chopped-up reptiles and other things that didn't feel right going into your mouth.

My first task was to drink maggots, mealworms and water

all sloshed up together. I held my nose and gulped it down. Next, I found myself looking into a cup of blended fish eyes and pig eyes, but I had to pass on that one. The thought of it was just too disgusting.

I forced myself to eat a thick cookie with dead cockroaches embedded in it and live cockroaches running all over it. The cookie would have been quite tasty if not for the cockroaches, but it was really dry and the idea of eating bugs made me gag. My mouth had to be empty before I was allowed to drink any water and it was really hard not to be sick as I tried to swallow all the bits.

I managed to drink a cup of blended crocodile parts next (oh, my God, argh!) but couldn't face eating four long fat water worms out of a glass – I was convinced they'd get stuck in my throat. Jenny and I shared the horror of the last dish: I drank a cup of slimy yellow witchety grub mixture and Jenny ate a live, fat, wiggling witchety moth grub.

It was all so gross. I cried my eyes out on the walk back to camp. I felt completely humiliated.

So, yes, I was really happy to get out of *I'm a Celebrity . . .* When I got evicted on my tenth day, I was over the moon. 'Oh, man, thank God for that!'

Back at the hotel, my chaperone gave me back my dud phone. 'Thanks,' I said, putting it into my pocket.

She looked at me expectantly. 'Don't you want to switch it on?'

'Nah, I'll look at it later.'

'You don't want to phone anyone?' she screeched.

'It's not about the phone,' I said coolly. 'I prefer to connect with people in person.'

She gave me a strange look.

'Have you got my suitcase?' I asked, because, of course, that was where my real phone was.

'Yes. You'll get it later,' she said.

My heart started racing. I was desperate to call Aidan, but I had to keep up the pretence. 'Can I have my suitcase as soon as possible, please?' I asked. 'I've got some clothes in there that I really want to change into.'

I was so glad to get back to the UK, and when I finally moved into my new home, I thought, What I had to do to get into this house!

Was it worth it?

At last I had a lovely garden, and in that garden I had a little shed, which I made into a little kiddie cave for Aidan. It was so, so sweet. We had a really nice community around us and I had fantastic neighbours: the woman living opposite us kept four chickens in her tiny garden and used to bring me six eggs every single week; Pat across the road took my parcels in when I was at work; and the lady next to her was a local optician, so she would bring Aidan's glasses to him when they were ready. There was also a house in the street that offered sheltered accommodation to adults with disabilities and one of the guys who lived there always used to come and give me a hug when he saw me. Bless him. 'I love you, Alison,' he used to say, and I'd reply, 'I love you too, babs.'

So, yes, it was definitely worth it, because I was happy as a lark, doing my job and coming home to my little three-bedroom semi, literally five minutes around the corner from my mum. I was exactly where I wanted to be.

Strictly

I didn't regret taking part in *I'm a Celebrity . . . Get Me Out of Here* but one of the lessons I learnt from it was to try to do shows I know I'll enjoy. And four years later, when I was invited on to *Strictly Come Dancing*, this wasn't even in question. 'We've had an enquiry from *Strictly*—' my agent said.

'Say yes!' I shrieked, before she could finish. 'Yes, yes, yes! Is it a definite offer? Oh, my goodness, who do you think I'll get as a partner?' And I was off imagining myself in a world of dazzling dancing and shimmering swirls.

I felt as if I'd already won the show when Tess announced at the launch that Aljaž Škorjanec was to be my dance partner. I danced around in joy screaming, 'It's Ali and Ali!'

Aljaž is such a lovely man, a fantastic teacher and the best dance partner I could possibly have had. We were so happy and excited to have each other. Aljaž had been with Abbey Clancy the year before and he'd won with her – but I was completely different from Abbey and it was going to be a different sort of year. We went on to have an absolute blast.

The only thing that disappointed me was that we didn't do any lifts in any of our dances.

We tried doing a lift once and Aljaž went bright red. I could tell he nearly died with the strain of it. 'Babes, I can't put you through this,' I said.

'No, no, no, we can do it!' he insisted.

'We're not doing it. I'm too heavy.'

'Don't worry – you can lift me!' he suggested.

But the first time I tried to lift him I swear the biggest fart ever flew out of my bottom! I have never been so embarrassed in my life. Imagine farting in front of Aljaž, not only the most stunning guy you've ever seen but also the best professional dancer in the world! He looks like he's not heavy, but it almost killed me when I lifted him. I nearly had a hernia. And I'm strong, too.

'Listen,' I said, my cheeks burning up, 'I don't ever want to lift you up again. Let's never talk about what just happened. Please, don't tell anyone.'

'Don't worry about it,' he said.

I was mortified. I might think about letting one go in front of a boyfriend after I've got to know him quite well, but not Aljaž – never. He's like a god!

My first dance on *Strictly* was a cha-cha to 'Every Woman' and I loved every moment of it. My dress was one big sequin with tinsel streamers that sparkled every time I did a twizzle. The theme of our routine was 'The Bodyguard' – with me as Whitney Houston and Aljaž as Kevin Costner. At the start of the routine, Aljaž had to unhook the rope that led to the dance floor and I'd make my entrance through a curtain to 'I'm every woman . . .' Only he was so nervous that he couldn't unhook it, so there was

a bit of a pause. Come on, Aljaž, you can do it, I was thinking – and he did, just in time. Phew.

'*Viva la diva!*' Bruno cried, when we'd finished the routine.

'You're infectious. I'm never going to get bored of
watching you,' Darcey Bussell said.

Even Craig Revel Horwood praised me!

I was thrilled that the dance had gone so well, but my
left ankle was in a lot of pain afterwards. 'I don't know
what it is,' I told Aljaž.

'You should go to the doctor,' he said, 'just to get it
checked out.'

I put my feet up when I got home, but the following
day, when I was back in action rehearsing the next dance
with Aljaž, I was in agony again. So I went to hospital to
have my ankle X-rayed.

Back at home, I had a phone call from the radiographer.
'You need to come back to the hospital and pick up some
crutches. There's something wrong with the tendon in
your left ankle,' she said.

My heart started thumping. 'You what?'

'Come back to the hospital, because you need crutches.'

'Okay, thank you!'

I put the phone down and left it at that. I kept it a secret
because I didn't want my *Strictly* career to end.

I'm not sure what I did to it, but my left ankle has never
been the same. If I exercise on it, I'll sometimes get a
shooting pain up the bone. If I go for a walk, I have to
turn round and come back home after an hour. If I'm not
pounding it all the time, then it's fine, but if I walk too far,
I know about it.

I struggled during the whole of *Strictly*. The judges kept saying, 'Alison, that left leg is very lazy.'

I'd do the dance and then be in absolute agony afterwards. Only Aljaž knew, because I didn't want people to feel sorry for me, or think that I was trying to get more love. I just wanted to do *Strictly* – but my left ankle wanted to go on holiday.

We found a way round it: Aljaž would show me the dances and I'd sit on a chair and learn them by watching him. I was quick at picking up routines but didn't get enough practice doing them because I'd only want to do it a couple of times before my ankle got fatigued and gave way.

I especially liked the routines where we told a story through the dance. Our foxtrot in the second week saw me dressed as a high-powered office worker, wearing glasses, with my hair tied back quite severely; Aljaž was my personal assistant, wearing a striped shirt and braces, and I was the boss. We strutted around the dance floor doing a right old fandango – well, foxtrot, actually. I loved it: I was in charge!

'Darling, those hip swings created a sonic boom,' Craig said, when we went up for the judges' comments.

By the time week three arrived, I needed to take it easy because of my ankle. Unfortunately, we were doing the jive so we did a sort of 'jive lite' and I just about managed to get through it.

'I don't think it was your dance. I think you found it difficult,' Darcey said, and she was spot on, because I had another problem with the jive, in that my boobs did their own dance while my legs were jiving. This was my lowest-scoring routine.

The next week was better, because we were doing the samba, where there's more emphasis on moving your hips and you don't have to jump up and down as much.

'You've got your mojo back this week. Well done,' Len Goodman said encouragingly, and it was one of my highest-scoring dances.

Our tango was great in week five, because it was another character dance and I really got into playing the part of the haughty lover.

I was thrilled when Bruno declared, 'That was like watching an opera!'

Aljaž and I had worked to bring out the melodrama in the dance and it had paid off.

I didn't smile once that week because it wouldn't have worked with the drama of the dance, but I made up for it the next week by beaming all through my American smooth to the Kate Bush song 'Wuthering Heights'. At the start of the routine, I was lowered to the floor on a trapeze bar swing wearing a beautiful soft white dress. How romantic! It took strong stomach muscles to get off that swing gracefully but I felt absolutely wonderful as I floated through the routine in my lovely dress, while Aljaž guided me around dressed as Heathcliff. This was my favourite dance. I don't know why. Maybe it was because I was flying through the sky on a trapeze, or because I loved the dress so much – I loved everything about the dance. It came to me so naturally – I didn't even have to think about the steps as I swirled around the floor.

Side note: this was one of the dresses I kept from *Strictly* and later wore when I 'married' The Rock. Yes,

Kevin Hart 'married' me and Dwayne Johnson in that very dress! So I have two very special memories of wearing my beautiful 'Wuthering Heights' outfit and, who knows, maybe there'll be a third one day – at my real wedding!

But we were in the bottom two that week, which was horrible, and our survival depended on the results of a dance-off with Scott Mills and Joanne Clifton. Even though I was glad to have a chance to float through the dance again, it was incredibly nerve-racking to think that everything came down to this one performance. Then disaster struck when, midway through the dance, my sleeve flapped over Aljaž's face and he couldn't see where he was going. It only lasted a moment or two, but it led to me having a hysterical fit of laughter once we'd finished. It struck me as so funny that my sleeve had got caught on his face that I Just. Couldn't. Stop. Laughing. It really tickled me. Then the judges and audience started laughing too and soon I was doubled up and gasping for air. It took every ounce of control I could muster to compose myself for the results – and I was very relieved when the judges saved me and Aljaž.

Our final dance the following week was the Charleston to 'Friend Like Me' and our outfits had a black and gold tuxedo style that looked really flattering on both of us, especially me. Craig said the dance was very stylish too, so I was happy. My problem wasn't with the steps or the rhythm: my boobs just seemed to take on a life of their own while I was dancing. I'd find they were doing the cha-cha while my hips were doing the Charleston.

Unfortunately, we were bottom of the leaderboard again that week and back in the dance-off – this time against Caroline Flack and Pasha Kovalev. As soon as I heard it was Caroline I was up against, I knew what the outcome would be and it made me a little tearful. In my mind, there was no doubt that Caroline would go through because she was such an amazing dancer. Meanwhile, Aljaž was disappointed because he felt we'd done such a great Charleston, so neither of us felt great.

Caroline was a really lovely person, bless her. 'I want you to get through, Alison!' she kept saying.

We wanted each other to go through, but it wasn't a surprise when 'the two Alis' had to bow out. Still, we went out on a high and Aljaž gave me a lovely kiss that almost made up for it! He was a fantastic partner in every way. He did my shoes up for me at rehearsals and carried my bags for me whenever we went anywhere. He was the perfect gentleman.

I definitely had the *Strictly* blues for at least two weeks after we left the show. Imagine going from working so closely with someone to absolutely nothing. Stopped. Zero. I was really upset. So I was overjoyed when I found out that I'd been asked to do the *Strictly* tour. Travelling to arenas around the country with the *Strictly* crew was a dream come true for me: I'd be reliving the whole *Strictly* dream.

However, it was a completely different experience from being on the show. We were living out of a suitcase and staying in different hotels every single night. What I loved about it was that we all travelled around in the tour bus

together – and most of the fun happened on those jour-
neys. There was always lots of joking and bantering and all
the naughty ones sat at the back: Simon Webbe, Mark
Wright, Thom Evans – and Aljaž. I'd be in the seats halfway along chilling out with Frankie, Caroline, Joanne and
Scott. It was like being back at school, to be honest with
you – we were like a load of kids travelling round having
fun on an extended school trip.

Some days weren't so good: I missed Aidan loads when
we were on the road and my ankle kept playing up. Luckily,
we had an amazing physiotherapist on tour with us who
kept icing it for me and – this is quite weird – the pain used
to disappear the moment I peeped out from backstage and
saw the sea of smiling faces in the arenas. Zap! Ankle pain
completely gone.

After the *Strictly* tour came the *Strictly* P&O cruise, which
was every bit as good as the tour. It took us to Gibraltar,
Madeira and Portugal over four days and nights, and all I
had to do was dance a couple of numbers with Aljaž,
which was brilliant, and host a couple of quizzes and really
fun evenings. The rest was holiday and chilling out: going
to the sauna and the gym, swimming, eating and having
fun with all the *Strictly* professionals.

It was amazing to be around all the *Strictly* fans: people
who really enjoyed the show and were eager to know
every little behind-the-scenes story. It was a fantastic trip
for them, because they were able to speak to the dancers
and see Craig Revel Horwood in all his glory. The dancers' costumes were on display so they could touch and
feel the *Strictly* tassels and glitter and see the shoes. They

also got to meet one another and swap ballroom dancing and *Strictly* stories.

I can honestly say that, for four wonderful days, life was a pleasure cruise for us all.

Love lessons

It was around the time I was doing *Strictly* that I met my last significant boyfriend and he was lovely, a real gentleman. We were compatible in a lot of ways. There was just one problem: my mum didn't like him.

Mum was someone who wore her heart on her sleeve: if she loved you, you could practically see the outline of her rose-tinted glasses when she looked at you; if she didn't like you, you'd know about it purely from the expression on her face. She was very clear about her intentions.

One boyfriend made the mistake of going to Mum's house to tell her how much he liked me. 'What do you bring to the table?' she asked him pointedly.

He hadn't known how much he had to impress Maria!

Mum and I were so close that her opinion really mattered to me, and if she didn't connect with one of my boyfriends it had a major effect on me, which was a real shame. I'm determined not to make the same mistake with my son when he starts dating. If I don't like who Aidan chooses to be with, I won't show it. I'll try my hardest to let him live his own love life.

It didn't work out with my last boyfriend – and not just because we didn't have my mum's blessing. To be honest,

I'm not very easy to be with. I'm not the best at calling back or texting. My friends get it; my family gets it. They know I can't text or phone them when I'm working. They understand that when you give your best to your work, your loved ones can sometimes lose out. If you get home and you're feeling tired, maybe you don't want to chat; maybe you don't want to go out for the night; maybe you're writing a book (because I'm an author now); maybe you just want to chill and be boring.

In my job, you're constantly on call, especially when you first start out. I remember a Friday morning when one of the top producers at *This Morning* phoned up: 'Alison, we want you in New York. We've booked you on a flight at five o'clock this evening.'

I looked at my watch. It was 11 a.m. 'This evening?'

'Yes. You need to be at the airport by three o'clock.'

I had to drop everything and ask my mum if she could have Aidan for the weekend. What made it worse was that it happened to be my mum's birthday. Gutted. 'I can't come tonight because I've got to go to New York,' I told her.

'Babe!' Mum said. She was so understanding. 'Go for it. I'll look after Aidan. Don't worry, we'll have a lovely time.'

My mum was just so supportive of my lifestyle. She was amazing and I don't think I could have done this job without her. But she was my mum, not my boyfriend – and it's difficult if you feel you're being side-stepped when you're in a relationship. Sometimes I think it's just easier to be single in this job.

Maybe I need to pay more attention to my love life and give it a chance, because I do meet the most wonderful men – I meet wonderful men, and then I mess it up. We always manage to stay friends, though, which my girlfriends find weird. But if you still get on and there are no hard feelings, why not be friends? Life's too short to bear grudges.

I'm proud of these friendships, actually. It shows I'm a good judge of character. I've never had a psycho. (Well, I've had psycho moments, but that was on my side of things!) I don't have stories of someone stalking me – I'm the one who stalks them! – or anything horrible happening. And none of my ex-boyfriends has ever sold a story. Although, to be fair, it's probably because the sex was so good that there isn't a story to be sold, lol.

We can learn from our relationships and I think I'll learn from the mistakes I've made. I see people sharing absolutely everything about their boyfriends and husbands on Instagram, but I'm quite a private person and have never wanted to reveal too much about the people I love. However, in my next relationship, maybe I need to show my boyfriend how much I love him by declaring it publicly to everybody.

What a scary thought.

Cringe.

9. TAKING UP SPACE

It's often said that obesity didn't exist in the Stone Age – I've heard that a lot. People probably didn't give much thought to body image and weight back then, either. It was feast or famine, and if you could bulk up on mammoth meat during the winter months, you were doing well.

Our relationship with food is so much more complicated, now that we don't have to go out and hunt or forage for our mid-morning juice and snack, and however good the ancient berries and seeds tasted, those cave people didn't have a clue how delicious a Terry's Chocolate Orange is. But I bet there was at least one overweight person back in the Stone Age, you know. Come on! There's always one or two – and what are the chances that I'm somehow related to them?

I'm mostly happy with the way I am, but I've also asked myself why my body is the way it is. I've often wondered whether there's a reason why I'm bigger than other people, and if perhaps it's something I can trace back to childhood, or a life experience I haven't properly processed. Maybe you'll understand why once you've read this chapter, which is all about me and my body.

Crunch time

It was 2007 and, as I was sitting down to interview Matt Damon about his third Bourne film, *The Bourne Ultimatum*, I noticed that my chair felt a bit tight.

I know, I was interviewing Matt Damon! What can I say? Hottie! Fittie! He was incredible. I was so pleased to meet him.

But halfway through the interview, something awful and embarrassing happened. My size and weight went against me and suddenly the side of the chair broke. It was a horrible, shameful moment. My girth had broken the chair while I was interviewing Matt Damon, one of my idols! I was mortified. I wanted the world to swallow me.

'Are you okay?' he asked. He was very nice about it. 'Let's get you another chair.'

I'm a Black woman, but I went bright red in the face. 'Don't worry about it,' I said, and I ripped the arm off the chair and flung it onto the floor.

That made him laugh and, instead of bursting into tears, which would have been the natural thing to do, I started laughing as well and we carried on with the interview.

'That was so funny,' my producer said afterwards.

But I was mortified. 'If you don't mind, don't show that part on TV,' I said.

'Okay,' he said.

'Right, that's it. I'm having a gastric band,' I decided.

I didn't want to be fat any more. I didn't want to be big and stand out. I wanted to be smaller. I wanted to be tiny.

Diets

Reporters often want to talk to me about diet and weight, but they're asking the wrong person, really. I'm the last person to get advice from when it comes to diet, exercise and being slim because I don't know how to be slimmer. I still haven't learnt how to do it.

In the last twenty years, I've tried every diet going and none of them has made the impact I was hoping for. When I lose weight, I often don't know how I've done it. It can just happen when I'm not thinking about it: I get slimmer. Then I get bigger, and I don't know how that happens, either. It just does.

I've always been big and I don't know why. The only way I can explain it is to say I'm one of one. We're all unique. This is how my body works. It doesn't follow the rules.

The rules are confusing too. You'll get a rugby player with a high BMI, but he's fit as anything. Of course he's going to be bigger – he's a rugby player. Men have denser bones than women; bone density varies among different races and Black people have denser bones than White people, so I don't see how you can apply the same BMI rules to everyone.

I know for a fact that every body is different because I

live it. I'm a big girl but I'm not sitting gorging on food all day long. I haven't got the time. I see people who do gorge on food all day and they're not fat. If anything, maybe I need to eat more food, more often, to make my metabolism work better.

The diets that have worked for me are the ones where I've been smashing food the whole time. I've done Slimming World – bloody hell, I never stopped eating! I did Weight Watchers as well and I've never eaten so much in my flipping entire life. It's like you eat yourself slim – and yet it's hard for me to shift more than a few pounds.

The last time I lost weight in a big way I was twenty-one, when I ate soup for lunch and a baked potato for supper every day for four months. What was fascinating was how differently people treated me after I lost the weight – and over the years I've often noticed how people change around me when my weight fluctuates. On the one hand, I find that when you're smaller people are more interested in what you've got to say – they want to hang around you more. On the other, you're more of a threat to people, especially women. I find it so interesting.

But why haven't I been able to lose a significant amount of weight since I was twenty-one? What has changed? Is it my fault?

I'm not a big eater but I'm not going to lie: I love sweets and I'm addicted to sugar. I don't drink. I don't smoke. I don't do drugs. I do chocolate, lol. Leave me with something, guys! Leave me with my flipping chocolate! It's my only vice. I'd rather eat chocolate than anything, and not any old chocolate, but the best: Terry's Chocolate Orange.

My problem is that once I start eating a Terry's Chocolate Orange, I can't stop because I love the taste of it. Instead of having two segments, I'll have five, maybe ten, when two should be enough.

I don't doubt that I could give up chocolate and still be happy. Once I put my mind to losing weight, I'm all over it. I'm at the gym all the time; I'm on my healthy food. I eat sweets only every now and then. But often it doesn't make a difference, which doesn't seem fair. If I can't lose weight, what's the point of dieting?

'Oh, stuff it,' I'll say, unwrapping a Terry's Chocolate Orange.

Eat your dinner

Could it be that my size and weight are somehow tied up with an experience I had early on in my life? One of my strongest childhood memories is of a Sunday when my dad came to the house and we were sitting eating our roast dinner together. My mum's great cooking came into its own when she made her Sunday roast, but it reached a point when I'd had enough to eat. 'I've finished, Mum. I don't want any more,' I said, even though there was still food on my plate.

'All right, then,' Mum said.

My dad looked up. 'Eat the rest of your dinner,' he said in a stern voice.

I shook my head. 'I've finished. I don't want any more.'

'Eat your dinner now.'

His eyes bored into me – and then he started taking his belt off.

Now, I'm not sure whether he was serious or just putting on a show to scare me, but my mum looked at me wide-eyed, as if to say, 'Oh, my God!'

My eight-year-old self did a quick calculation: if my dad beat me with his belt, my mum would try to protect me and he would overpower her. I'm going to have to eat this food, I thought.

To keep the peace, and out of self-preservation, I ate every last bit of my dinner.

A few years ago at a charity lunch, I sat next to a therapist who made a connection between my size and that Sunday when I was eight. When I explained what had happened, he suggested that I've carried that moment through my life ever since.

I went away and thought about what he'd said. It made a lot of sense to me. I never leave anything on my plate, and that's maybe one reason why I'm a big girl. That Sunday lunch left a psychological imprint: I finished my food to protect myself and something about that experience set up a lasting link in my brain between eating and self-preservation.

Once you make a connection like that, you should be able to do something about it, and I think I've let it go . . . up to a point. For instance, my son doesn't get into trouble for not eating all his food. If there's food left once he's satisfied, I chuck it away, or he chucks it away. As for me, after my chat with that therapist I went home and had a Terry's Chocolate Orange. His wise words had left me feeling so depressed that I sabotaged myself again.

Torture

In 2007, after *that* Matt Damon interview, I had a gastric band operation. Physically, it worked – it created a pouch at the top of my stomach that filled so quickly I couldn't eat much. But mentally, I wasn't ready for the drastic change it made to my eating habits. It didn't feel right to be eating so little, and although having a gastric band is supposed to make you feel full quicker, I was eating salad and still feeling hungry afterwards. This is hell. This is absolute torture! I thought. I haven't eaten enough! It was confusing.

Then something started going wrong physically: I was sick a lot. I couldn't keep anything down. It was really distressing. I felt as if my body was rejecting the foreign entity inside me and I began to get ill.

I kept it for two years, until it was getting to the point where I couldn't even keep down one bite of food. I can't take this any more, I thought miserably. I'm striving to have a slimmer body and I'm not happy. I'm vomiting all the time. It's awful.

I went to see my surgeon and told him what was happening. 'Let's get you in and have a look,' he said.

But I'd made up my mind. 'I'd like you to take it out, please.'

Normally, it takes fifteen minutes to remove a gastric band, but it took my surgeon an hour and a half because so much scar tissue had grown around mine – so thickly that it was squeezing my stomach shut to the point where I couldn't eat anything, which was why I was always being sick.

The weird thing was that, in all that time, I didn't lose more than a stone. Can you believe it?

'Why am I constantly battling to lose weight when my body doesn't seem to want to get rid of it?' I asked myself. 'Maybe I need to embrace who I am and just be me. Do the exercises I love to do, go walking, go to the gym and just carry on being who I am. Maybe if I stop fighting and trying to lose it all the time, the weight might come off easier.'

I wish I could tell you a great story about how I went on to lose all my weight after that, but I can't. I was a lot happier and felt freer, but unfortunately I put weight on. It was to be expected, because I wasn't being sick all the time and had more room in my stomach. The mystery was, why hadn't I slimmed down in the two years that I'd had the gastric band?

It was several years before I found any kind of answer to this question . . .

Crisis

In 2009 I hit another wall, when I was asked to take part in a BBC TV gameshow that was being filmed up in Scotland. I hit it literally, figuratively, metaphorically and every other possible way you can hit a wall. And in the process I learnt a valuable lesson.

Hole in the Wall was hosted by Anton du Beke, and the team captains were Joe Swash and Austin Healey, the rugby player. The aim of the game was to stand on the edge of a swimming-pool and contort your body so that you could get through different-shaped holes in a polystyrene wall as it moved towards you. If you didn't make it, splash!, into the swimming-pool you went. And that was the fun of it, because it wasn't easy getting through the holes.

All the contestants on this show had to wear silver boiler suits. Before I went up to Scotland, the wardrobe department asked me what my size and measurements were, so I measured myself meticulously and sent them the information they needed. I was confident that I had measured myself correctly, but when I got to the studio and tried on my suit, lo and behold, it was the tightest silver boiler suit you've ever seen. It left nothing to the imagination. It was literally showing off every ounce of my body.

When I looked in the mirror, I was mortified: there was no getting away from the fact that I was massively over-weight – and I just had to deal with it. I had always been good at hiding my size with the cool clothes I purchased, but now the true Alison Hammond would be exposed in all her glory for the world to see. The live audience was going to see my big body. The contestants were going to see it. The team captains were going to see it. The people in the gallery were going to see it.

I felt horribly self-conscious and nervous. 'Is there any-thing you can do?' I asked a seamstress in the wardrobe department. 'Can you add some more material so it's a bit baggier?'

She shook her head apologetically. 'It's far too late in the day, I'm afraid. You'll have to make do with how it is.'

The producers could see I was definitely not feeling this outfit and didn't want to do the show. I was used to feeling confident – invincible – before I went in front of a cam-era, but not today, in Scotland, miles from anywhere, miles from home, in a skin-tight silver boiler suit. For the first time in my TV career, I felt vulnerable.

But I couldn't pull out of the show. That wasn't me. I was never that person who called their agent and walked off set. A massive frog filled my throat and tears welled in my eyes. 'Control yourself, Alison. You're a professional,' I told myself.

My heart was sinking but it was also racing. I felt heat around my head and started to sweat. I felt as if I was worth less than everyone else. I didn't want to be inside my own skin and I didn't want to go ahead with filming the show. I couldn't do it: it was too exposing. I felt naked for all to see.

Just at the moment I was about to call Becca, my agent, and beg her to get me out of it, Joe Swash burst into my dressing room with the biggest smile on his face. 'Hello, Sexy, look at you! I love it!'

He gave me a big hug and I could tell by his face that he didn't care one little bit what I looked like. He was just glad to see me. 'You're on my team and you look amazing!' he said.

That was the moment when I knew I was going to be okay. Joe had suddenly given me confidence and he didn't even know it. We looked such a pair standing there in our silver outfits that I smiled and thought, This is me. Let's make the best of this situation. Let's overcome this feeling and make people smile.

I made peace with the idea that, although I didn't have the best-looking body, it was my body and an amazing body at that – after all, it's been with me all my life. 'People will probably smile, maybe even laugh, but then they'll move on,' I told myself – and that was exactly what happened.

I went into the corridor, where people from the production team smiled, laughed and then carried on. I went to meet the other team players, who greeted me, smiled, hugged and then carried on. I think everyone was far more worried about how they looked than what my silver suit was doing for me.

Why was my ego so big that I thought the whole world would be staring at me? 'Al, chill your boots. You ain't that important, babs,' I told myself.

The thing is, people do stare. They make a judgement and then that's pretty much it. They move on. That's what we human beings do. Once you actually get this, you can pretty much overcome those times when you don't feel good about how you look. I started to feel more and more confident. If I can wear this silver boiler suit and no one is even bothered, I can do anything, I thought.

The show started and we made an entrance by slipping down a slide. Unfortunately I got stuck midway, but Joe Swash quickly ran over to me and pulled me down by my feet, which was the best thing he could have done. It was very funny, but also he actually rescued me because I was moving nowhere fast.

I'll never forget what Joe did for me that day, and how he made me feel. He'd instinctively known that I was nervous when he'd come to my dressing room and was kind enough to put me at ease, which helped me find my power within. Now he had released me from the clutches of the slide.

After that, I had such a good time that I forgot what I looked like. I was in the moment, enjoying myself: we made the shapes for the holes in the wall; we cried with laughter; and we fell into the pool. Not one person was bothered by the way I looked: I'd created this whole 'reality' that was totally unreal and unnecessary. I had one of the best days ever and I'm so glad that the way I looked – or felt I looked – didn't stop me living my best life.

What I learnt that day was this: people are people and they will always look at you, but they are more worried about themselves than they are about you. So, don't stress if you want to go to the gym or swimming-pool: just go. People will look and then move on. Lower that ego and live your best life. Your body is an instrument, not an ornament.

Smaller than

I haven't conquered being the ideal slim person, but over the years I've come to think that I'm beautiful the way I am. I look great in clothes and I love my big, hanging, saggy tits. My friends call me 'Superboobs' because my boobs are so amazing.

When I'm on my own, I don't even think of myself as big. I just think I look lovely: I've got a lovely shape, a nice face and I like my skin. Even when I take my clothes off, I think, You're all right, actually.

It's only when I see myself standing next to someone on TV that I'll think, Oh, my gosh, I'm really big!

I think I must have a kind of body dysmorphia that means I don't notice how big I am until I'm actually next to someone else. It's the opposite of anorexia. I don't look in the mirror and think, Oh, no, I'm so fat, I look in the mirror and think, I'm beautiful, man. I look so good. I look fire.

Why are we destined to be smaller, anyway? Yes, health is important, but everyone's obsessed with being smaller. 'Look at the size of your waist! You look so amazing in that outfit. Look how tiny your feet are!'

We're all trying to fit into this box that not everybody

can fit into, and if you're one of those people, you need to create your own box. We're not all the same and we never will be. You can only be yourself because everybody else is taken.

Why are we so obsessed with being small? It's in women's heads to be smaller, to be *smaller than*. Our thinking has been controlled from the Day Dot. We've always been made to feel we should be small in every sense, verbally and physically.

'I can't go out with him because he's too short! He needs to be taller than me.'

Why does a man need to be taller than you, if you love him? All the men I've been out with have been smaller than me. We're all the same size horizontally! So why does it matter? Love is love.

Often when I meet people, they say, 'Have you lost weight? You look smaller today.'

Why can't they just say, 'Al, you look nice today!'

Why does that question have to be attached to it: 'Have you lost weight? You look smaller.' What does it really matter?

I'm clever at putting on clothes that make me look good. Some days I might look smaller. Other days I might not. I can't understand why it's so important for people, either way. Why can't we take each other for what we are, as individuals? I am what I am. Does it really bother you that I take up a little bit more space in the world?

Even if you'd rather be smaller, I think you need to embrace who you are at the time. I see so many people who won't do certain things because they feel too self-conscious.

Like the people who won't go swimming because they don't feel nice in a swimming costume. You won't go swimming? Swimming is such a lovely thing to do! And it makes you feel so good. So why won't you go swimming? Literally, you're going to stop your life because you don't feel good in a swimming costume and people will be looking at you? It's so sad to think you'd let that stop you. Don't let your ego get in the way.

As I learnt when I did the TV show *Hole in the Wall*, people are doing their own thing and going about their own business. They don't really care. They might look at you, then look away and get on with their lives. That's it. We need to shrink our egos, or at least put them aside and think, You know what? I just want to go and enjoy myself. I want to go on holiday and wear that bikini.

I say, 'Wear the bikini'! Let your big flabby stomach hang over it! In my mind, you're 'beach body ready' whenever you flipping well want to go to the beach. If you want to wear your bikini, wear it, and if you want to go on a diet, go on a diet.'

In the spring of 2021, I was filming in Brighton on one of the first warm, sunny days of the year and all of a sudden I just wanted to go swimming, so I went into the water with my clothes on and had a good time. When I watched it back on TV, I thought, How embarrassing! Why did I do that? But in the moment I loved it.

While I'm doing something, I'm in my body enjoying it, looking from the inside out. If somebody else is looking at my body, thinking, Look at her! that ain't my problem, is it?

It's not my business, it's their business if they've got a

problem with my body. Because I haven't got a problem with it and I'm going to enjoy myself in that moment. If I see myself in a photograph afterwards, I might think, Oh, no! I look terrible! But while I'm doing it, I'm having a good time. And do you know what? I've learnt that people are not so much mean to others as mean to themselves. So, honestly, don't worry about a thing. Get out there and live your life.

A week or so after I went swimming with my clothes on, I was doing a punting section for *This Morning* with Josie Gibson in Cambridge. The day before, the producer texted, 'I know we're not supposed to ask ladies this, but what size are you and how much do you weigh?'

There and then, I decided I wasn't going to be stressing about how heavy I was for the punt. I can swim. I've got all my lifesaving badges from when I was a kid, I thought. I'm going to be all right. Let's just go with the flow.

'Just get me the biggest life jacket and we'll deal with it tomorrow,' I said.

Life is so short. I want to have all these lovely experiences and enjoy them.

PTSD

Humans are complicated, aren't they? And their relationship to weight and size can be complicated too. So hear me out when I say that having body positivity doesn't mean you don't also have your vulnerable points: although I love my body and think it's absolutely beautiful, like everyone else I can be a little bit sensitive about it sometimes.

It may sound crazy, but whenever I hear the word 'elephant', it takes me straight back to being at school and the nasty comments the boys used to make about me. It's like a trigger word: when I hear someone say 'elephant', I instantly think they must be talking about me.

Anything to do with elephants sets it off. I remember it happening when I was on safari once. Some elephants came into view and I had heart palpitations because I was worried that someone was going to say, 'Alison, look! An elephant, like you.'

It happened again at a charity event I went to with Kate Lawler. Now, Kate is very good at doing the red carpet. Wait, did I mention that I don't like red-carpet events? I'm not keen on all that attention and the photographers shouting your name. 'Look over here, Alison! Look up.'

It's the one thing about my job that I've never enjoyed.

I don't know whether it's because I haven't got the body everyone wants you to have, or because I don't like how false it feels. I've been on the other side of it as the reporter interviewing people and seen how ruthless the press are and how they treat people. So often, a reporter will be talking to somebody but not really listening to them because another, better-class celebrity is walking down the carpet. It makes me want to treat everyone exactly the same when I'm on the press side.

Whether you're A-list or Z-list, you're just a human being as far as I'm concerned. You're doing an amazing job and I want to find out about it. So if Brad Pitt rocks up and everyone's attention turns to him, I just carry on speaking to the celebrity I'm with until I've finished.

I've got into trouble for it in the past. 'Alison, you've just missed Brad Pitt!'

'Well, I was talking to this other person . . .'

'Yes, but Brad Pitt just walked past.'

I expect that's why I've never really enjoyed walking the red carpet myself, although I'm quite an extrovert and I like being on television. It's got to the point where I will actually avoid it and come late or go through the back entrance.

I don't know many celebrities who enjoy walking the red carpet, and if you do, I don't know how, because it's weird and bizarre. I find it really cringey, standing while someone takes photos of me. It makes my skin crawl and I never really like the pictures when I look at them afterwards. They always get the wrong angle and I always end up hating the picture. Nah, red carpets are not for me.

There is one red-carpet photo I like, of me and Holly

Willoughby, where I'm clinging to her and the photographer has captured a genuine sense of 'I'm so happy to see you!' We weren't posing or trying to be anything that we weren't. We just let it happen in the moment and it's a lovely picture of us both laughing and appreciating the fact that it's just crazy being on the red carpet.

Going back to the event I was at with Kate Lawler, it was a ceremony to honour animals and I was giving out one of the awards, with Ricky Gervais and Brian May from Queen, the guy with the big hair. Brian May was sitting at a table in front of us with his lovely wife, Anita Dobson, who played Angie in *EastEnders*.

Me and Kate hadn't seen each other for absolutely ages and we were eating our dinner and having a great old time while the ceremony was going on. When Kate and I are talking, the whole world could disappear and we wouldn't notice. 'What have you been up to?' 'Got a new boyfriend?' 'What's happening?' 'How's Aidan?' It was a chance to have a really good catch-up.

So we didn't notice a band coming onstage to perform – we were too busy gossiping and chatting. Suddenly, Brian May turned to us and said, 'We're trying to listen and I can't hear a word of the singing. Could you please keep your noise down? Have some respect.'

We instantly stopped talking. But you know when you've been told off and you're a little bit giggly? 'Oh, my gosh, we just got told off by Brian May from Queen!'

Things got worse when the band left the stage. Brian May got up to make a speech and started off by saying, 'Now, there's an elephant in the room, isn't there?'

Oh, no, I thought, he's just told us off so he must be talking about me!

I had a full-on panic that he was going to start embarrassing me in front of everybody.

'He's talking about me, Kate!' I whispered.

'Of course he isn't. Don't be stupid,' she said.

'Now, there's an elephant in the room, isn't there?' he said. 'We're at a ceremony for an animal charity and there's meat on the menu. But there shouldn't be when we're doing an event for animals. So why is there meat on the menu?'

Relief washed over me. Thank goodness for that! I thought.

When it was time for me to give an award, I couldn't help getting up onstage and telling everyone that we'd just been told off by Brian and I'd thought he was talking about me when he mentioned the 'elephant in the room'.

'Of course I wasn't talking about you!' he said afterwards. 'I just really wanted to hear the singers and you were being too loud.'

I'm not sure what lesson I took away from that day, but I'm sure I'm not the only person who lives with PTSD dating back to their schooldays.

'Be kind!' I'm always telling Aidan.

You can never unsay the things you've said, and you just don't know how hurtful they might end up being or how long they will stay with the person.

Clumsy

I spend a lot of time dressing to distract from my size, but occasionally I use my size to my advantage on TV because I am a little bit clumsier than other people and it can be quite funny to watch. I sometimes sense that I'm not going to fit through that gap without knocking something over, but I'll do it anyway because I know it's going to make good TV. It's me being naturally klutzy, like I've been since I was a kid, only I won't try to hide it or take extra care, like I do when I'm round at a friend's house.

Other times, it's a total accident, hand on heart. I'm thinking of the day in 2018 when I was doing the weather forecast in Liverpool Docks as part of our celebrations to mark thirty years of *This Morning*. This was a tribute to the floating weather map they'd had in the late eighties and I was standing on a floating map of the British Isles with two gorgeous models dressed as sailors.

After I'd walked up and down the map, pointing out where it was going to rain in Great Britain, I had to leap over a small gap to get to Northern Ireland. And because I sometimes don't realize how much weight is behind certain movements, that motion of me jumping across to Ireland was more forceful than I'd expected.

Unfortunately, I bumped into one of my helpers and he bedonged into the water. 'Oh, my gosh, are you all right? I'm so sorry!' I shrieked, as he clambered back onto our floating island.

'It's gonna be a little bit wet in Northern Ireland, as you can see,' I said. 'I'm so sorry, babes. Anyone got a towel?'

Criticism

Back in 2009, I was in the makeup room before going on a TV show when one of the presenters started talking about Twitter and how brilliant it was. 'What is it?' I asked. He explained it to me. 'I don't get it,' I said.

'Think about it,' he said. 'It's like having your own PR company. Say you've got a hundred people out there who love you to bits. On Twitter you tell them, "I've got a new book out," and with a press of a button the information goes to your hundred followers. Then they tell a hundred people and so it goes on until your book becomes popular.'

'Wow! That's amazing,' I said.

'Come here and let's set up a Twitter account for you,' he offered.

Within minutes hundreds of people were signing up to follow me. I could literally see my numbers on my Twitter account going up in front of my eyes. 'Look, you've got a hundred now,' my friend said. 'Two hundred . . . five hundred . . . You've got eight hundred. Hey, you've got a thousand followers now!'

It went up and up and up. I was absolutely amazed.

Social media has changed a lot since then and sometimes the comments are not very nice. I try not to let it bother me when I see a negative post, but occasionally there will be something that hits a nerve.

A few months ago, a woman put up a tweet that upset me. Afterwards I thought that maybe the reason it upset me so much was that she was expressing something I've thought myself.

Her name was Jo and she put: 'I know I'll be slated and I don't dislike Alison, but we need healthy role models on prime-time TV. This isn't right.'

I usually choose to stay silent when I read hurtful comments like that, but this time I put: 'Listen, I'm just human. I don't pretend to be anything else. #BeKind.'

It's true: I don't set myself up as a role model. I'm not trying to be anything other than who I am. It's also true that I don't drink, I don't smoke, I don't do drugs and I don't have frivolous sex with Tom, Dick and Harry. I've got a son who is my world and everything to me. I try to be kind and I like to help people whenever I can. So, I found it quite devastating for this woman to say I'm not a good role model purely because I take up a little bit of extra space in this world.

I had some lovely messages in response. One woman said: 'We love you, Alison . . . Please never change. You are a beautiful, warm-hearted woman.'

Another said, 'You put the yay into my Fridays. They have never been so great and uplifting. Love what you do, babs . . . Everyone deserves kindness.'

Someone else said, 'And Jo's a cracking role model, isn't she? Wow. We love you, Alison.'

And 'This is awful. I absolutely love watching you and

envy your job. You make me laugh and you're brilliant at what you do.'

And 'You're lovely, beautiful and bubbly, and nobody deserves to feel anything less than they are. Sending lots of love.'

The last comment nailed it. No one – no matter who you are, whether you're bigger or smaller, whatever colour you are – should be made to feel less by anybody, because no one is better than anyone else. We are all equal, and we all should be kind to each other and treat people with respect.

I really appreciated the support I got online, but that one snidey comment continued to trouble me. I thought, Oh dear, am I a good role model? Should I get a little bit slimmer, lose some weight?

In situations like this, I try to remember my mum's advice. 'Alison, just try your best and see what you can do.'

I need to remind myself that I'm human – I'm not perfect – and like everyone else, I have good and bad days. Sometimes, I will feel amazing and no one can touch me. I'll see a nasty comment and think, Your opinion doesn't matter because I don't know you and you are nothing to me.

Other times, I'll take something on board and it will bother me because it echoes what my inner voice has been saying to me. Ultimately, though, you've got to overcome challenges. So when the chair breaks and I'm opposite Matt Damon and it's highly embarrassing, or I have to put on a tight silver boiler suit and go on national TV, I will overcome it, because my personality is strong. Equally, I may struggle with the hurt I feel when people say nasty things about me, but I will overcome that trauma and move on.

My 'vice' is very visible, isn't it? Everybody can see my vice and they all have an opinion. It doesn't matter whether I've got hormone issues or whether there's something going on with my thyroid. They don't see that. They just see the size of me. 'Look at her. She must be lazy. What a terrible role model! She must just be eating all day long.'

In fact, I walk every single day. I've got 8-kilo kettle bells in my living room and when I'm watching TV, I'm pulling weights during the ad breaks. I make myself do ten dead lifts, then ten lifts of the weight, so that I can sit down knowing I've done some exercise. It's silly and a little bit OCD, but that's my thing.

My cholesterol is quite low because I don't drink and my blood pressure is like an athlete's. It's only my sugar that's a bit high. I'm also very strong when it comes to lifting. From an early age, I carried all the suitcases when I went on holiday with my mum. If the woman who posted that nasty comment needed to be lifted and carried out of a burning house, I'd probably be able to do it – I'm that strong.

This body is incredible. I've climbed the Atlas Mountains in Morocco. I've had a baby. I can do the splits. I'm double-jointed in my shoulders. So maybe you need to look a little bit deeper when it comes to judging my body, because it's got me through forty-six years of life so far.

A lot of people look down on people who are fat, but really and truly, their unkindness is often more about their own fear of getting fat. A few can be quite cruel, though.

I hate the way people think they can bandy about the words 'obese' and 'morbidly obese' just because they're medical terms. They feel it's justified to call someone 'morbidly obese' because they're using medical jargon, but it's not nice. I remember seeing Edwina Currie on TV making a reference to another guest being 'obese' and I had a strong sense that she was using the term to put her down.

'Obese' is a horrible word in my eyes. It's so demoralizing. I'd prefer to be called fat. Call me fat or overweight: they're descriptive words. Mind you, there's a new term now – 'super obese' – and I wouldn't mind that so much because I do actually think I'm super, lol.

Health

I may be up and down with my feelings when it comes to my weight, but I really mean it when I say that I love being big. I love myself and I love my largeness; I love big women and I love big men.

What I don't love is not being able to run.

Unfortunately, lockdown was dire for me in terms of weight. I couldn't control my eating or how much exercise I did, and I didn't have any desire to go on a diet. I just didn't care any more. It was so bad.

In the end I had to think, I'll eat what I want, because I need to be happy in that aspect at the moment.

I think it's known as 'covering'. I started eating to cover up – or try to pretend – that we weren't all locked up under house arrest during a global pandemic. Fat lot of good it did me, lol.

It wasn't a surprise to find out from my GP that my blood sugar was higher than it should have been. When she diagnosed me as pre-diabetic, I was actually pleased, because to me it meant I'd basically been told I wasn't diabetic, as I'd feared I would be. That's great news, I thought. It's wonderful news. She's saying I am borderline, but I'm not diabetic, so now I just need to make sure I stay not diabetic.

Something started to shift in me. I was still looking at myself and thinking, I am fine, but I was also conscious that people who are overweight run into problems as they get older, and that if I didn't address it, the likelihood was that I would die early. Usually, I would counter such thoughts by telling myself, 'Oh, well, we're all going to die one day, so it's about making your life amazing, taking each day as if it's your last and just enjoying it.'

And I stand by that – but life was becoming less enjoyable for me. By the time the second lockdown started to lift, I was really heavy, I was pre-diabetic and I wasn't walking very well because of the weight I was carrying on my back. Just imagine what I do in my life, all the travelling and rushing around, and I was carrying the equivalent of a fifteen-stone man on my back, every step of the way. Even cycling was out, because every time I went anywhere on my bike I'd get a flat tyre.

I wanted to change and was starting to accept, after years of trying, that perhaps I couldn't do it on my own. Maybe I need help, I thought.

Sometimes you need to put number one first, and when it gets to a point where your health is being compromised, you have to do something about it, if you can. But, first, I wanted to understand why it was so difficult for me to lose weight.

I went to see a doctor who specializes in weight-loss issues. 'Alison, it's actually not your fault that you can't lose weight,' he said. 'Your metabolism is different from most other people's.'

It was such a relief to hear him say those words. 'Really?

That's what I've been thinking,' I said 'Today I've had some melon for breakfast, a ham and spinach sandwich at lunch and I'll have some juice tonight, but I won't lose any weight. Why not?'

The doctor went on to explain how many different factors can impact a person's metabolism, from genes and childhood eating habits to your hunger hormone levels. Some of this was news to me: I knew my genes had an impact but not that I had hormones controlling my appetite.

Eating lots of sweet stuff doesn't help, obviously – I guess I knew that! And not being able to exercise as much as I'd like also slows my system down, so it's a bit of a vicious circle. How can I break it? I'm getting to a point where I would consider weight-loss surgery, but I'm still looking at my different options and wondering which direction is best for me. I've got a good life, but I love exercise, sport and feeling fit and I don't want to lose those possibilities, so I need to think seriously about what to do. I also want to live longer and feel healthy: I mean, if I die tomorrow, I've had a wonderful life and anything else is a bonus, but ideally I'd like another forty years of happiness and laughter.

I'm realizing that, ultimately, you can have a nice big home and all the rest of it, but the only house you ever live in is your body and you really need to look after it.

As I said, it's complicated! And Terry's Chocolate Oranges really are more delicious than anything else in the universe . . .

10. ON MY TRAVELS

Whether I'm working or not, I really enjoy travelling. Before every trip, I always say to my producers, 'I'm really looking forward to our holiday!'

'Alison, we are *working*,' they always remind me.

But, honestly, how is the audience going to enjoy it if you don't treat it as a holiday? Yes, we've got schedules to keep, but I don't see my abroad shoots as work. When I just get on that plane, train or boat I'm off to have some fun, man.

All sorted

What I love about my working trips abroad is that they usually only last a couple of days – four days maximum – but the amount of activities we pack into those days makes it seem as if we've been there for two weeks. Our itinerary is planned out to perfection and we have a fixer who makes sure we've got all our permits to film and smoothes the way. The timetable is precision: our meals and excursions are set out; we have breakfast here, lunch there, do this, do that. It's brilliant.

Yeah, I've seen Bordeaux now, I thought, after I toured the region in 2018.

What a brilliant few days that was! I went around markets and vineyards, learnt a bit of French and sampled some fantastic food and wine – and, for the first time in my life, I found myself liking wine. It genuinely felt like a holiday because I had so much fun: I rode bicycles and drove around in a classic car; I even had a naked massage with grape seed.

I might come back in the future but I don't need to, because I've literally seen it all, I thought, as I got on the plane home.

It was the same when I went to Madeira in the summer

of 2021. I did everything: I went on toboggans down the side of a hill, took a beautiful cable car ride, tried the local cuisine, went to the beach and swam in the hotel pool – all in forty-eight hours.

Some of my favourite trips have been to Disney World or Disneyland – I can honestly say that I've enjoyed them all. They're such super places and I've had a love for all things Disney ever since my mum took me to Disney World when I was thirteen. One of the things I appreciate most about Disney is that it's inclusive of everyone, unlike some of the other places you go to, so no matter how big you are, you can fit all the rollercoaster rides. I absolutely love rollercoasters.

Usually, I visit Disney to introduce the launch of a new ride, like the Twilight Zone Tower of Terror, but in 2018 I actually became a princess and helped to celebrate the eightieth anniversary of *Snow White* at Disneyland, Paris. It was a dream come true: the wardrobe team at Disney helped me to design a beautiful dress that was made specifically for me in light and leaf greens – and then I walked around Disneyland, Paris, dressed as a princess, totally believing that I was a princess. The real Snow White even taught me how to do a princess twirl.

Best day ever!

LA

People often talk about the phases in their life being a journey, a rollercoaster or a walk in the park. But I can't think of an apt way to describe the week I went to report on the Oscars in 2019, because it was off the flipping scale of metaphors about life. So hang onto your hat, because this is going to be a bumpy ride!

We started on a high, going straight from the airport and checking in to a cool, iconic hotel on Sunset Boulevard. It's a famous rock 'n' roll hotel where, in the late seventies, the drummer of Led Zeppelin would ride a motorcycle along the hallways, and in 1972 Keith Richards famously dropped a TV out of a window. I was there to make my own piece of history.

I love those fancy American hotels. As I go into my room for the first time, I'm always wondering, What's the bathroom going to be like? Has it got a rolltop bath? What's the shower like?

I don't like a fixed shower above my head because I don't wash my hair every single day. I like a shower with a detachable hose that goes around the body, so you can wash yourself without getting your hair wet. Why don't they have showers like that in America? What if you don't want to stand in the shower with your neck cricked back to keep your hair dry? Shower caps never really seem to work, either.

I like to have a pool and a gym in my hotel, even though I don't use them all the time. It's nice to know there is a gym where I can people-watch and do a little bit of tread-mill and cross-trainer, maybe a few weights. It makes me feel better in myself.

A nice breakfast buffet makes me feel less homesick in the mornings. For me, the buffet shutdown was one of the most annoying things about Covid. Fat lives matter as well, do you know what I mean? I was tempted to start a campaign to bring back buffets, I was missing them so much.

Anyway, in LA for Oscars week 2019, I checked into my room and, first things first, used the bathroom. Instantly the toilet got blocked. Ruined!

The toilets in LA are not that great – they really need to sort out the plumbing system, along with the showers. I don't think my poo was necessarily that big – it just couldn't get round the U-bend! It was annoying, because it meant I had to call down to Reception.

'Hello? My toilet's blocked.'

'No problem, we'll send someone straight up.'

A few minutes later, I opened my door to the most attractive man I have ever seen in my life. He was wearing shorts and a T-shirt over his tanned, fit body and carrying a toolbox. 'Hi, I'm from the plumbing department,' he said, giving me a five-hundred-watt LA smile.

There was literally a supermodel standing outside my room, come to unblock my toilet. I couldn't even look at him.

This is the worst day of my life! I thought.

'Yeah, it's just through there,' I said awkwardly.

I went into the bedroom and hid under the covers until he was ready to go.

'All done,' he called out.

'Thank you! Bye.'

Oh my god, earth, swallow me up!

Elton's party

Every year, Elton John holds an Oscars party to raise money for his AIDS Foundation. It's fantastic: anyone who's anyone and isn't at the Oscars goes to Elton's to watch the ceremony, mingle and enjoy themselves. I was invited to do interviews on the red carpet, along with my cameraman and producer. It was fairly busy, but we had a good position so there were plenty of opportunities to grab interviews with all the big names.

Unfortunately, my cameraman only had a pass for the red carpet, but me and my producer were lucky enough to have actual seats at a table inside the party – and not too far from Elton John's table, to be fair. The likes of Leona Lewis and Caitlyn Jenner were also invited: we were rubbing shoulders with some really big stars. Having seats inside meant we could go in and eat when nothing was happening on the red carpet, and then my cameraman would ring my producer and say, 'Elton John is arriving!' and we'd run out, do an interview, go back in and eat a little bit more. Then he'd phone us again, 'Paris Hilton's here!' and out we'd run again.

Sprinting in and out of the party wasn't exactly glamorous, but the whole vibe was exciting, what with the bouncers yelling, 'Show us your wristbands!', people wanting to see and be seen, film stars taking photos of each other, paparazzi cameras flashing, and the air changing when someone famous arrived.

At one point a PR came over. 'Just to let you know, we've got Taron Egerton arriving soon. Unfortunately, he's doing a very limited number of interviews and won't be available to speak to you.'

Elton and Taron had just collaborated on the movie musical *Rocketman*, directed by Dexter Fletcher, which was set to be released the following year and had already been tipped to be a serious Oscars contender.

'But Taron's the main event, apart from Elton!' my producer protested.

With all the hype that was building around *Rocketman* – and Taron's amazing performance as Elton – we were really excited about seeing Elton and Taron together for the first time. They were even going to be singing onstage at the party.

My producer wouldn't accept that we weren't going to be allowed to speak to Taron. She was like a dog with a bone. 'This is terrible. We have to interview him,' she insisted.

We saw Taron arrive and he was doing interviews along the red carpet. 'Sorry, you can't speak to him,' the PR stressed again.

'Okay, no problem,' I said.

I stood to the side and looked at the floor. Gutted.

Then, as Taron came along the red carpet, I heard my name being called, 'Alison!'

Taron was calling me!

'Taron!' I called back.

I'd never met him before but he seemed delighted to see me, absolutely beaming. 'I saw you making Hugh Jackman's year, the other day. That was cool,' he said.

Could this get any better? I thought. He's British, he's seen *This Morning*, and he's enjoyed watching me interview Hugh Jackman.

It was overwhelming; I went into a full-on interview with him.

Meanwhile, standing behind him, the PR was fuming. She couldn't say anything, because Taron had come to me and was practically fan-girling me, but she was giving me daggers.

Next, Elton and his husband, David Furnish, arrived. I'd never met them before and Elton was so, so charming as he talked about *Rocketman* and the work of the AIDS Foundation. We had a lovely chat on the red carpet, and then he said, 'Come here!' and gave me a kiss.

Me and my producer went back inside the party, where the Oscars were playing on a big screen while everyone enjoyed their dinner. After the meal, there was a charity auction and then the Killers played a private gig and we danced all night. Pixie Lott and Paris Hilton were both on the dance floor with us – it was the most glamorous mosh pit I've ever been in.

By the end of the evening, the gold strappy sandals I was wearing were absolutely killing me, so I took them off and left them at the side of the red carpet. The heels weren't high, but I'm not good with a heel, and I didn't miss my shoes because the red carpet was nice and squishy.

In all the excitement, I forgot where I'd put them and had to go home with no shoes on. I went to bed thinking they were lost for ever, but when I woke up in the morning they were outside my door. Result! The shoe fairy, a.k.a. my wonderful producer, had found them and whisked them back to the hotel.

What a star.

Thirty seconds of fame

One night, outside the Cadillac party at Chateau Marmont, the big pre-Oscars showbiz bash where all the Oscars nominees go, I experienced what it felt like to be a Hollywood superstar.

As we left the hotel, all these paparazzi and fans crowded round me, yelling, 'Alison! Alison!'

'That's weird – they know who I am. I'm famous in America!' I said to my producer, utterly amazed.

But as I walked over to greet my crowd of fans, they all ran past me and flocked around Allison Janney, who had been Oscar nominated for *I, Tonya*.

I was devastated. 'My' fans had deserted me! They didn't want to know. I'd felt what it was like to be a Hollywood superstar in LA – and it was taken away from me in seconds.

Once the other Alison had gone, a few of the fans came back to me. 'Come for the dregs, have you?' I said, giving them my autograph anyway. I'm not proud.

Massage

By the end of the week we were exhausted. We'd been working a million hours, filming day and night, going to parties, gifting suites and other Oscars events – and then I was having to get up and go live on TV at four o'clock in the morning, when it was midday in the UK. We were hardly getting any sleep.

On our last night, my friend Tammy phoned the hotel. I'd met her, a TV producer, through another friend; she was also out in LA covering Oscars week, working every bit as hard as I had. 'How about a nice relaxing massage to take away the stresses and strains of the week?' she suggested. 'Shall I pick you up at your hotel?'

'Brilliant idea,' I said.

We got into an Uber and asked the driver to take us to a spa where we could have a good massage.

'Okay,' he said. 'How open are you?'

'Really open!' we said, not really thinking through what this might actually mean.

He drove us to a spa in Koreatown, west of MacArthur Park, and we went inside and asked for two massages: I opted for a full body massage and Tammy chose a milk and fruit exfoliant treatment. So far, so good.

We were given a towel each and told to put on a little blue hairnet. Then an assistant led the way to the changing rooms, taking us through a main spa area full of women in little blue hairnets milling around stark naked with their big hairy fannies out.

It was one of those moments when you want to turn back, but you can't.

We were really polite to the assistant. 'This is where we change? Thank you. These are the lockers? Fantastic.'

But when she left us alone, we both had an uncontrollable fit of giggles. 'I'm so sorry, Alison! I've brought you to a naked sauna!' Tammy tittered.

We tried not to make a noise – we were like sniggering schoolchildren who were afraid to giggle aloud in case they were told off by the teachers – but we couldn't stop the laughter bubbling up inside us.

'Stuff this,' I said eventually. 'We look stupid standing here with clothes on.'

I undressed, got my boobs out and started posing up against the wall naked.

Now, I've never seen anyone laugh as much as Tammy laughed when she saw my big Black saggy titties dangling there. She wasn't subtle: she creased over laughing and then fell to the floor and curled up in a ball, screeching and giggling hysterically. To be fair, she says that it wasn't actually my boobs that made her laugh so hard, bless her, just the whole situation – and that I whipped them out so suddenly and started posing. Either way, the sight of my boobs usually has a massive effect on people, because they are superboobs. People love them. They have dreams about them for days after seeing them.

The assistant reappeared. 'Be quiet. You are disrupting other people's peaceful massages,' she scolded.

We tried to pull ourselves together and behave. But then, as Tammy knelt down and tried to open one of the lockers, a naked woman came in and started talking to us. It was very hard to keep a straight face during this conversation, because the woman's vagina was at the same height as Tammy's head, just inches from her nose.

A spa assistant gave me a weird nightie to wear and sent me off to my massage room. I lay on the massage table and waited. When my masseur came in and saw me on the bed, he let out a massive huff and groan, as if to say, 'Oh, for God's sake, look at the size of this one!'

He went on to give me a very vigorous massage, slapping me all over and throwing my boobs around. It was embarrassing and traumatizing – I couldn't wait to get dressed and go. I'd just wanted to have a nice, relaxing massage and instead ended up in the red room of *Fifty Shades of Grey*.

Meanwhile Tammy was having her milk and fruit exfoliation treatment in the next room. All I could hear was slap, slap, slap as her half-naked therapist hosed her down with milk. Next, she told me afterwards, she was told to lie on a table, where she had her face piled high with kiwi and mango and was hosed with more milk. By the end of it, she had so much fruit weighing down her face that she couldn't speak – or cry for help.

When I saw her back in the changing room, she looked broken. 'I feel traumatized,' she said.

I was nearly speechless. 'Oh, babes, at least you had a woman. I had a man!'

We got dressed and left as quickly as we could.

'I've never done anything like that before, Tammy,' I said, as we sped back to our hotel in our taxi. 'Can we pretend it never happened?'

Thread and dread

And so the day arrived when we were going home. We had worked hard and everything (well, almost!) had gone really well. My only problem, if you can call it a problem, was that I'd been given so many free goodie bags at the Oscars parties that I couldn't fit them all in my luggage. 'I'd better go and buy another suitcase,' I told my producer.

'Okay, but remember we've got to leave for the airport at six o'clock to get our flight,' she said.

I looked at the clock by my bed. It was only eleven, so I had loads of time.

'Do you want me to come with you?' she offered.

'No, don't be silly. I'll go on my own.'

I went outside our hotel and hailed a yellow taxi, which took me to a luggage shop in downtown LA, where I bought a suitcase. As I was coming out of the shop, I noticed a brow lounge just along the street. My eyebrows were looking really bushy, so I thought, Might as well go and get my threading done.

I went over to the taxi driver, who didn't speak English very well. 'Are you okay waiting for me?' I asked.

He gave me a thumbs-up, so I put my suitcase in the boot and went into the threading shop.

While I was in there having my eyebrows done, a guy came into the salon. 'Can I use your toilet?' he asked the manager.

'No, we haven't got one,' she said.

Ooh, that's a bit strange, I thought. There probably *is* a toilet in here, but she doesn't want him to use it.

I took another look at the man. He was tall, slim and Mediterranean-looking, with stringy black hair. There was something a bit dodgy about him and I could sort of see why she didn't want him using her facilities.

He left the salon and I thought nothing more about it.

I paid for my threading, and as I was walking back to my waiting taxi, I saw the man who had just asked to go to the toilet hovering on the pavement, talking to my taxi driver. I got into the back of the car and the taxi driver came round to the front, got in behind the wheel and started the engine. Just then, the man who had been in the salon slipped into the passenger seat.

My taxi driver turned to me and said, 'Is okay. We drop him on the way.'

I wasn't completely happy about it, but I said, 'Okay.'

'Are you on vacation?' the guy in the passenger seat asked me as we pulled away. He spoke with a Spanish-American accent and stank of weed, which is legal in LA.

'No, I'm not,' I said.

'Are you working?'

'Yes,' I replied.

I was being quite curt with my answers and I could see that it was getting his back up. 'You don't really wanna talk to me, do you?' he said.

'It's not that. I'm just wondering why you've got into the car.'

'Relax, I'm going to be dropped off on the way. I'm not going to hurt you.'

My heart immediately started to race. Why would someone say that? I thought. Why would someone say, 'I'm not going to hurt you'?

My instincts were on alert: Alison, something's not right here.

As we drove along, I thought, I'm going to have to try to befriend this guy.'

'So, what do you do?' I asked him.

'I don't do anything,' he said. 'I'm not a good person.'

My stomach contracted. Why wasn't the taxi driver clocking any of this? Was his English that bad?

'Why aren't you a good person?' I asked.

'You don't wanna know,' he said.

I was hating this journey now.

The guy got out his phone and started to make a call. 'I wanna speak to my lawyer,' he said, into the handset. 'Is that my lawyer?' he went on, and I couldn't tell if it was a real call or if he was pretending. 'Listen, I just want you to know that I'm about to do something *infamous*. Everyone is going to know me for what I'm about to do. It's gonna be bigger than anything.'

Oh. My. God.

I instantly assumed that he was planning to kill me and the taxi driver.

What am I going to do? I thought in a panic, going through my options in my head. I could get out of the car and make a run for it, but I'm not a fast enough runner. I could scream for help, but if he's got a gun he might shoot me on the spot . . .

My thoughts swung all over the place. 'Oh, what have I done?' I asked myself despairingly. 'I've had a lovely time here with my producer and cameraman. I've worked hard and done a good job. I've been on the telly. And now, just for the sake of taking a few freebie bits and pieces home to England with me, I've come out on my own to buy a suitcase, got into this car and I'm going to be murdered. I'll never see my family again. I won't see Aidan again. I'm such an idiot!'

The guy in the passenger seat was still talking. 'This is going to be so, so good. It's gonna be the best day of my life,' he gloated.

I went into protection mode. 'Oh, gosh,' I said to him. 'I'm really looking forward to seeing my son when I get back home. He's fourteen and we love each other so much. And my mum – I can't wait to see my mum, as well.'

'I'm not sure that's gonna happen today,' he said, turning to give me a menacing smile.

I swear my heart stopped beating. I was eyeballing the flipping driver in the mirror, trying to signal him with my eyes – 'Can't you see he's a lunatic? We're going to die!' – but he seemed completely oblivious to what this guy was saying and doing.

We drew up at some traffic lights. I'm going to have to get out of this car and run, I decided. There's nothing else for it, even if he chases me down, even if I don't know where I'm going. Otherwise, I'm going to die today, in LA, because if he's got a gun on him he's definitely going to kill me.

My heart pounding like crazy, I quietly tried the car door. It was locked.

The guy in the passenger seat swivelled to look at me again. 'Why are you trying to get out of the car? Are you worried? Are you scared?' he asked, with a low laugh.

'Why would I be scared?' I said, not meeting his eye.

He smiled. 'Trust me, today is a big day. I'm going to be *infamous*.'

I took out my phone, my heart in my mouth, and tried to ring my producer, but I couldn't make a call without Wi-Fi. I'm a dead woman, I thought, slumping back in the seat. I started crying, silently. I'm going to lose my life here.

Finally, we stopped at the hotel. The taxi driver got out of the car and the guy in the passenger seat got out the other side. He's going to pull his gun and shoot me now, I thought.

The car door lock released and I got out of the taxi and legged it into the hotel, leaving the suitcase behind me. The taxi driver rushed after me. And the other guy? He, Just. Walked. Away.

Inside the hotel, I burst into tears. 'Did you not see what that guy was doing?' I said to the taxi driver. 'He was going to kill us!'

The taxi driver shrugged. He didn't understand. Suddenly I realized that the guy in the passenger seat had just been trying to scare me.

And he had scared me – almost to death.

I ran up to my producer's room and stammered out what

had happened. I was shaking all over, a complete bag of nerves. 'Guns are legal here . . . People get shot all the time . . . You see it on the news . . . I thought I was going to die . . . I kept thinking about Aidan!' I sobbed. 'Oh, Aidan!'

She was shocked and worried to see me so upset. 'Oh, my goodness, Alison, you poor thing!' she kept saying. 'Shall we call the police and make a report?'

'No . . . I don't want to make a fuss. I don't even want to think about it any more,' I said. 'Also, getting the police involved might delay us and I just want to get on that flight home.'

I was tearful for the rest of the day, and all the way to the airport, for the entire plane journey and in the car back to my house, I had one thing on my mind: I just wanted to get home to my son and hold him tightly in my arms.

And what a beautiful big hug that was.

Top flight

On the flight home from LA, I bumped into Dexter Fletcher, who directed *Rocketman*. We were flying with British Airways and we'd both been put in business class.

I was absolutely loving it until we were up in the air and I discovered that the front bit of my seat, where you put your feet up, was completely broken. Suddenly, it wasn't like being in business class, after all; it was like being in an economy seat. I was devastated.

'Is everything okay?' one of the stewardesses asked me.

'Yes, great, except you can't put your feet up on my seat, because it's broken,' I said.

'Oh dear!' she said. 'Don't worry about it. Let me see what I can do.'

The next thing I knew, she upgraded me to first class! It was my very first time in first class, so I was excited.

'I don't think my seat's working,' Dexter joked.

I turned to him and smiled. 'See you later, babes!'

She showed me into first class and put me in a beautiful first-class seat. Jennifer Hudson was behind me. Ri-Ri was in front of me. Yes, Rihanna was in front of me. I couldn't believe it – we were like the Three Degrees! Me, Rihanna and Jennifer Hudson, on a flight: I actually felt like I was famous, like I was somebody.

I kept getting up to go to the toilet, but really, I was having a look at Ri-Ri close up in her first-class seat (on the way to the toilet) and Jennifer Hudson (on the way back). I nearly started singing, 'And I am telling you I'm not going . . .' and 'Work work work work work work . . .'

How cool is that? I was literally milling with the stars.

Italy

Life doesn't always go smoothly when I'm working, but my adventures in Pisa in the summer of 2019 took things to another level – and that level was chaos.

I was on a Disney cruise for *This Morning* when I stopped off in Pisa in Italy to present a competitions segment. My first surprise was how overwhelming it was to see the Leaning Tower. Believe me, when you see it up close, you instantly want to take the classic picture that everybody takes, pretending to hold it up.

Before I went to Pisa, I used to see those photos and think, That's so clichéd! But when you get there, you think, Yes, I want to do one of those too!

Joe Swash was with us and we were all just having a good time. We had a fixer, a local person who looks after you when you're filming: he or she sorts out your travel, your security and your permit to film. We were good to go and everything was sorted. We were all ready to film our segment in front of the tower.

But for some reason the Pisa police had it in their heads that we didn't have a permit to film there – even though we did – and the fixer and the police started having an argument literally at the point we were going live. It was a bit alarming, because I could hear the police behind me shouting, 'Do not film in front of the Tower of Pisa!'

Shouting the loudest was an especially ferocious female police officer. 'We can't go ahead. That policewoman is going to come over,' said my producer, looking worried.

'Do not pull the plug,' I begged. 'Don't lose this link. We'll do it now.'

At that very moment, I could hear Holly and Phil in my ear introducing my segment: 'We're going live now to Pisa with Alison. Morning, Alison! Tell us about the competition.'

The kerfuffle behind me was still going on as I started speaking – and out of the corner of my eye, I saw the female police officer coming for me. Now, she had it in for me. I had no idea why, but she had it in for me in particular, and I could sense her approaching as I carried on talking to the camera.

I tried to get to the end of the competition, then threw back to Holly and Phil: 'Oh, gosh, I'm going to get arrested. Love you loads. Laters.'

This Morning cut to a video about the Disney Cruise. Phil and Holly came back to me just as the police officer was having another conversation with our fixer about this permit.

'I'm actually shaking,' I said. 'If you just turn around and see the policemen, they hate me.'

The camera turned.

'No, don't!' Holly and Phil yelled. 'Leave it.'

The next thing I knew, the police were running towards me and I thought, You know what? I'd better leg it.

I was scared. I didn't want to get arrested. Now, I'm not the fastest of runners, but my legs could run that day and I just went for it and ran off.

At first, I was the only one running, but then my producer and my cameraman started running. 'This is so bad,' I gasped. 'Why won't they leave us alone?'

The police didn't give up. They kept following us, saying, 'Get away from the tower!'

Leading the charge was the policewoman who had it in for me. 'You! You!' she kept shouting. Obviously, she didn't have much English, but she could say, 'You!'

Why just me? I thought. There are other people here, you know.

I started thinking she had a grudge against my colour, because I was the only Black person there and she was picking on me. I didn't mention it to my crew – it was just a sense and I didn't want to make a big deal about it.

Eventually, we went back to the square where, lo and behold, right in front of the Leaning Tower of Pisa there was a hotel. 'Why don't we go and get a room in that hotel?' I suggested.

We got a room in a plum position and it only cost fifty euros. I couldn't believe it because, I swear, the one they gave us had to be worth a thousand euros a night. The window opened onto a beautiful view of the Leaning Tower of Pisa.

When I popped my head out of the window, I could see the police officers down below, still looking for us. They seemed really angry.

'We need to be careful,' Janice said. 'They're not messing around.'

We did the second link for the competition out of the window – and there was something so *Bourne Identity* about the situation that I did it with a blanket over my head. I was in disguise! 'The police are just down there, but don't worry, we've got this beautiful view of the Leaning Tower of Pisa,' I said.

By the third link, our fixer had sorted out the misunderstanding, the police had apologized, and we were allowed to go outside. But for about thirty minutes there, I felt as if I was Bourne on the run.

It really was a bit scary. Just from the look in that policewoman's eye, I had a strong sense that if anyone was going to jail that night, it was me.

So, there you have a few snapshots from my album of travels around the world. As you can see, there's never a dull moment. Unless I find myself in a taxi with someone who starts pretending to be a murderer. Or being chased down the street by a policewoman on a mission to arrest me, for that matter!

11. THE LAST LAUGH

I'm not saying anything new here but life can be tough. It's something we all know, especially after the horrors of 2020 and 2021. But somehow you've got to find a way to keep going when the worst happens. My way is to lean on my family and friends – and even make new friendships. Yes, I do mean you, Dermot O'Leary!

I think you've always got to find a way to keep smiling and take pleasure in life, even when it feels as if the dice are loaded against you. I've had quite a lot of resistance to deal with in recent years (trolls, I'm looking at you!) but I've made the choice to stay positive and focus on the people and things that are really important to me.

There have been extreme highs and lows, along with the endless flipping boring lockdown days that we really don't need to go into too much. Here's how it's been for me – and the lessons I've learnt . . .

Mum

I sometimes get the feeling that people think I live in a happy bubble all the time. It's not true: I'm human, so I'm not always happy and I'm not always nice. (Well, I am always nice, but some days I'm nicer than others, lol.)

I try being the best possible version of myself that I can be, but I'm sure there are days when I've been upset and found it hard to smile, and someone might have thought, Oh, gosh, she's a bit moody.

They don't know what's going on behind that moodiness, or what's happened to cause it, but if they think of their own lives, they can probably remember times when they haven't been at their best or brightest either.

I don't think I smiled much in the days after my mum told me that she had been diagnosed with cancer, on 13 September 2019. It was such a shock. I couldn't get my head around the idea that anything could happen to take her away from me. She was my core and my strength, my wonderful, kind, joyful mum. I just couldn't imagine life without her.

I wasn't the only one who loved and needed Maria: everybody she knew loved and needed her – and she was such a people person that she was constantly surrounded by her friends and family, even when she was really sick with cancer.

Mum wasn't the sort of person who just wants a call. 'Come over! Come and sit with me,' she'd say to people, and everybody came.

Maria was the glue that kept the family together. She was the person who would pick up the phone and ring all our aunties abroad, the person who put pen to paper and wrote letters to family and friends, the person who sent birthday presents and cards to the youngsters in the family. She was the one who brought everybody together for parties and barbecues – and then she'd get the caterers in because she wanted to make it extra special. She didn't do it because she had to: she did it because she wanted to, in happiness.

I kept a close eye on Mum after she was diagnosed. I was always looking out for her. One day over Christmas, I noticed that her temperature was too high so I called an ambulance and went with her to Queen Elizabeth Hospital in Birmingham. Mum was diagnosed with sepsis, which is also known as septicaemia or blood poisoning. Straight away the doctors put her on antibiotics and admitted her.

Mum's bed was in bay thirteen and there was a number thirteen above the headboard. I'm not normally superstitious, but I remember asking, 'Does she have to have this bed?'

'It's the only one available,' I was told.

I'll never forget that number thirteen above my mum's bed. I hated it. I don't know why they have number thirteen in hospitals. They should miss it out and just have twelve straight to fourteen.

Mum responded well to the antibiotics and was getting better, but then she took a turn and died on 13 January 2020, with her family around her. It was so unexpected.

Saying goodbye to my mum broke my heart. It still breaks my heart just writing these words on paper, pure and simple. Even now, it's tough for me to think about how painful it was, and still is. I loved her so much.

As I was leaving the hospital, a woman came up to me and said, 'Alison! Alison! Can I have a photo?'

I'll be honest with you: I really wasn't in the mood to have a photo with this woman. But I thought, You know what? It will make this woman happy. It'll make her day.

So I stopped and did a photo with her, even though it was six o'clock in the morning and my mum had just passed. And I smiled in the photo, but behind that smile there was such deep sadness.

'Oh, thanks so much!' the woman said happily.

I was glad to have brightened her day, but my heart felt very heavy as I walked away.

Thirteen again

Everybody who knew my mum was devastated when she died, because they were all touched by Maria. Not only that, but she was a really good cook, so people remembered her food and missed that about her too. It was a really big thing that they were never going to taste my mum's food again.

It's a massive loss for our family, because there isn't anyone else who's bringing us all together the way my mum did. Most of her generation is dwindling now. We're losing the strong Black women of our family and wider community. So now I have to step up and into Mum's shoes and try to be that strong woman.

My sister, brother and I helped each other through the days after Mum died. I don't know how I would have coped without them. We wanted to bury Mum on 14 February, but we couldn't get the church she wanted, so we thought, Well, she died in bed thirteen on the thirteenth of January, so let's just bury her on the thirteenth of February.

And that was the day we buried her.

I'm not a fan of the number thirteen but generally I try not to be superstitious. If I see ladders, I will walk underneath them: I don't want to be the person who won't walk under a ladder. I was brought up in a Christian family and my mum disapproved of superstition, yet I love anything to do with star signs now, and I get a lot of pleasure from reading my angel cards, which are designed to offer encouragement and guidance from the heavenly realm. I reckon I've got some kind of angel light within me: whenever I do angel-card readings for people they always say I'm completely right. And all I'm doing is pulling cards for them and reading what the cards say!

My mum didn't approve of the angel cards. 'Stop being silly. It doesn't work. I don't believe in all that,' she'd say – and then I'd do hers and she'd smile, as if to admit secretly, 'Yeah, that's definitely right!'

Friends

From the moment we lost Mum, it felt as if the world would never be the same again. And, weirdly, it really wasn't. Mum died in January, we buried her in February, and then the whole world changed in March. It really did feel like a catastrophic chain of events. I was kind of glad that Mum wasn't around to see the world in lockdown, though. I don't think she would have enjoyed being cooped up and I would have hated not being able to visit her.

Five months after my mum had passed, my dad died. Can you believe it? Suddenly both my parents were gone. 2020 wasn't a good year for most people, but I lost my foundations, and then my lovely brother-in-law, Andy, passed in early 2021, bless him, so we had the worst twelve months as a family, a lot of heartache. But, you know, we're strong, and we've come through it. We have faith and we're very tight as a family, and that brings us through.

As well as relying on my wonderful brother and sister during these difficult times, I also reached out to my friends. My lovely, kind friend Emma helped get me through my mum being ill and dying. She was incredibly supportive and I was so grateful to her. Sarah, from my Airtours days, helped me through a lot, and Josie, another really important friend, got me through the whole lock-down experience.

My friendship with Josie dates back to when I watched her win *Big Brother* in 2010. I was just a fan at that point, but thought she was amazing and could imagine us getting on well: I'd love her as a friend, I decided. She seems like a girl's girl.

A year or so later, I met her on a red carpet and was literally star-struck. 'I love you!' I burst out.

'I love you, as well!' Josie said.

We beamed at each other. It was a mutual thing! We exchanged numbers.

We stayed friends online, and then Josie invited me to go and see her in Bristol. While I'd normally say, 'Thanks, but I can't,' I said, 'All right, I'll come.'

I drove down to Bristol and we had such a good time. We went to the cinema. We went to the market. We bought a juice and went for a wander. I had the best day ever. Josie really makes me laugh. We spoke a lot about blokes – you know, men who had treated us badly, and why did we always fall for these fools? That was our thing and it's still our thing now. When we're not putting the world to rights or discussing where we are spiritually, we talk about men. We stayed in touch and our friendship grew.

Me and Josie helped each other through the first lock-down, when we were both very fearful of this new disease, Covid-19. It was scary because no one seemed to know what was going on. It was literally: 'Oh, my God. What is happening to our world as we know it? Are we going to die?'

Me and Josie spoke to each other all the time – we

probably phoned each other three or four times a day. It was a comfort more than anything, because Josie's a single mum and I'm a single mum and we understood what the other was going through. Our friendship helped us survive that really bad time – and, as they say, there is nothing better than a friend.

(Unless it's a friend with chocolate.)

Black Lives Matter

Along with the rest of the world, I watched the murder of George Floyd by a white police officer on 25 May 2020 and, along with the rest of the world, I was left shocked and bewildered.

About a week later, a campaign called 'Blackout Tuesday' swept across social media, protesting against racism and remembering the Black people who had been killed by police. It was featured on *This Morning*: Phil and Holly phoned me to ask me to give my point of view.

I literally went on air within seconds of their call, so my words – and my tears – came tumbling out of me spontaneously. I'm kind of glad I didn't have time to think before I went on the programme because I wanted to get it right and probably would have over-thought it.

'First, I'm a mother to a fifteen-year-old Black boy,' I said. 'So when I saw that image of George Floyd, I saw my brothers, I saw my father, I saw my son. I saw everybody's son, and I was disgusted to my core. And it hurt me to the pit of my stomach to think that this is 2020 and we're seeing that.

'And let's be honest, this has been going on for ever – my whole life, my mum's life, my father's life, everybody's life.

And I believe that this movement, Black Lives Matter, is so very important. And it's so wonderful when I see my white and my Asian brothers and sisters standing by Black Lives Matter because it means they understand – they can't understand fully but they understand what we are going through as Black people.

'And don't get offended when I say Black people, because I'm not trying to offend white people. If you are offended by it, then you need to look within yourself. Appeal to your basic instinct of goodness.

'It's not about All Lives Matter – obviously we know that [all lives matter]. It's all about the fact that, if Black lives mattered, we wouldn't be in this situation now.

'So when Black lives matter, then all lives will matter.'

Afterwards, I was in bits. It was such an emotional time and all I could hope for was that I'd said the right thing. Instantly, my phone started pinging with texts.

Later, when my son said, 'That was great, Mum,' I knew I'd done okay.

Every person with compassion in their heart could agree that George Floyd's murder was wrong. But when it comes to talking more generally about racism and issues affecting people of colour, things become more complicated. My experience of being Black isn't the same as the next person's, and not all people of colour agree with each other. We're multi-faceted human beings. I can only speak from my own experience – and obviously I have experienced racist incidents throughout my life. I don't dwell on them, though, and I'll tell you why I don't want to go there: it's because talking about it is trauma. When you relive stuff like that, it's traumatic. So I'd just ask people to accept and believe that it has happened.

My biggest bugbear is when people say, 'I don't see colour'. To me, I find that is the biggest insult because when you say I don't see colour, it's another way of saying I don't see racism, I don't see injustice, I don't see inequality and I don't see you.

I want people to see me for who I am. I want people to see how my experiences have shaped my life. I also want people to see my character, ability and potential.

. . . And the fact that I'm really good in bed. Lol.

Even explaining the basics of being Black is actually quite difficult. That's why Black Lives Matter was set up: to show the disparities between Black and white people in all the different areas of life. On Blackout Tuesday, there was a chance to acknowledge that people of colour don't have the opportunities that white people have. Once we realize the truth, we can do something about it and things might change. I hope they do.

Trolls

My mum really cared what people said and wrote about me.

'Mum's been reading what people have been saying about you on Facebook again,' my sister would tell me.

'Just tell her not to read it!' I'd say.

Mum never mentioned it to me. She never said, 'I read this, and they said that,' but she took it all on board if people were nasty about me. According to my sister, she would sometimes write back under an assumed name and say, 'You don't know what you're talking about!'

Mum was very sweet like that.

As I've become more successful in my career, there's been a rise in online abuse aimed at me. It comes and goes, but some of the comments have been really nasty and I've come to see that you can't please everybody.

When you get trolled, your ego starts to take over and it's not a nice feeling. You want to answer back and you want to stand up for yourself, but you have to lower that ego and think, Step back, take a deep breath. This isn't about you, Alison. This is about how they feel, so let them say what they've got to say, then move on and enjoy your life because, ultimately, that's what we're here for.

Social media is fantastic in so many ways, but it bothers

me that people can say any nasty or upsetting thing they want to and get away with it. Their insults are like daggers: they can kill people. Words can really do damage – people have taken their own lives because of the hurtful things that have been said.

Sometimes I wonder why you have to say anything at all. If you were in a library or community centre and you saw a sign on a noticeboard offering 'Piano lessons, £20 an hour', would you put up a note saying, 'I don't want piano lessons'? Would someone else come along and put up a note saying, 'Your piano stinks!'? Maybe you don't need to make a comment. Maybe you can see the notice, 'Piano lessons, £20 an hour', then walk on by.

You might think, Hmm, I might do that, or No, I'm not interested in that, and off you go.

You don't have to put your two pennies' worth in and stick up a notice saying, 'You're crap at teaching piano. I wouldn't come to you for piano lessons if you were the last piano teacher in the world! I'm going to kill you and your piano . . .'

Why would you do that?

But in recent times, people have been very verbal online. Some of the messages I've had are vile. There was a period when I was being racially abused and it was very hurtful, especially as I always thought I'd transcended colour in my job. I didn't think my colour was an issue; I thought that they just loved me, Alison Hammond.

It was a wake-up call. It made me think, Alison, you are a Black woman, and you are representing, so own it.

And I always will own it.

I've had people saying, 'You're only where you are now because of the movement Black Lives Matter.'

Like I should be ashamed of that!

If I'm successful because of Black Lives Matter then the movement has done what it was supposed to do. I'm Black and proud. I always have been and always will be. I'm proud to be representing Black people. It's who I am.

And I know in my heart that I deserve every success. I know how much graft I've put in over the last twenty years working in television: the early mornings, the sacrifices, not being with my son enough, not being able to read him a bedtime story at night, not seeing my family, missing out on birthdays and parties, jetting off here, there and everywhere, sacrificing looking after myself – not going to the gym enough, not eating the right foods due to working so hard. I know that I deserve everything that's come my way. I believe that everything that happens in life is meant to be.

The one thing that hit me badly was seeing myself referred to as 'a Black host' in a tabloid newspaper headline.

Wow, that is really cutting, I thought, when I saw it. Look at how my colour is a thing! They haven't even used my name, Alison Hammond. I've literally become the colour of my skin. How upsetting is that? I'm not even my own name any more.

It made me mad to the point where I thought, I'm going to keep on doing what I do even if, ultimately, I'm never going to be everyone's cup of tea. I'll do it for my son and for everyone else who's been put down. And I'll enjoy all the opportunities that come my way.

So that's what I've done: I've enjoyed myself and I intend to keep on enjoying myself.

I don't often read what people have to say any more. I'm just doing what I'm doing and enjoying the vibe of what feels good on the day. If I've had a good show, then I'm happy as Larry. If no one else has enjoyed it, that's up to them and, of course, there are lots of other channels they can watch. It's not difficult for people to turn over.

There are lots of things I don't watch on TV, but I don't go on Twitter and say, 'I'm not watching that! It's a load of rubbish.' I just keep it to myself and I don't watch it.

The irony of all this is that some of the people who used to troll me now say that they love me. It's bizarre. People are so fickle, and it makes me think, Stop trying to please others.

Just please yourself and do what's right for you – what feels right – and you always know what feels right because it's in your gut. Follow your gut and do what's right for you. Our whole lives are about trying to please people: we start off trying to please our parents, our teachers, our peers. At what point do you say, 'Enough, now! I can't please you all. I need to do what I need to do'?

I think it comes with experience and adulthood. Stillness is also a key part of it. Having all that stillness and silence during lockdown made me think about what's important. Do we really need to please other people when they're living their own lives? Does it matter how many followers you've got? They're not really following you, are they? They're really not! I'll go with my own feeling of whether something's good or bad online: I post and go.

Sometimes I'll have a flick through some of the comments, but I don't religiously read them all, if I'm honest.

I measure the value of something by the way I feel about it. If I've had a good show, then it was a good show. Obviously I hope our viewers enjoyed what they've been watching, but I try not to worry too much about what other people think. It may sound harsh to say so, but it's how I protect myself. Reading horrible messages all the time is not good for anyone's mental health and I've got to protect mine.

I think the day you realize you don't need to please people is the day you realize you're free. You just need to please yourself, and I don't mean that in a selfish way. It's just that, however hard you try to please others, the truth is that you're never going to please everybody. It's impossible. It's not going to happen.

It's much better to listen to your heart and do what you think is right. At the end of the day, when you look at yourself in the mirror, the only person you need to make proud is that person staring back at you.

Black history

After I said my piece about Black Lives Matter on *This Morning*, I had a call from Sue Walton, a producer at ITV, and while we were chatting, it struck me that there was a lot of Black history – my history – that I didn't know about or had forgotten. I told Sue about the time that me and my mum had gone to see *Black Heroes in the Hall of Fame*, a musical theatre production about Black history at the Birmingham Arts Centre. Billed as '5,000 years of Black history in one night', it was an incredible show – with great music too – celebrating the achievements of more than seventy-five Black pioneers.

For me, aged fourteen, *Black Heroes in the Hall of Fame* was my first taste of Black history and the amazing Black inventors and artists who have changed the world through the ages. It was fascinating to learn about people like Mary Seacole, a British-Jamaican nurse who cared for soldiers during the Crimean War, and Garrett Morgan, the guy who invented traffic lights and the gas mask. It was the first time I'd ever heard about these people and what they'd done, and I was literally blown away by it. I kept wondering why my school wasn't looking into this side of history. I found it bizarre.

Black Heroes in the Hall of Fame had a real impact on me and my mum. We loved it so much we went back the following night and saw it again!

Did you know that Britain had a Black Roman emperor? I know – can you believe it? Septimius Severus rose through the ranks to take power and by AD 193 he was emperor of the whole Roman Empire. Who knew that?

Did you know there were Black people in Britain during Tudor times? There was even a Black trumpeter called John Blanke, who played in the court of Henry VIII. What's more, when John Blanke decided he wasn't being paid high enough wages and petitioned Henry for more money, Henry gave him a pay rise.

Also, I never knew that Henry's first wife, Catherine of Aragon, had an entourage of Black servants when she arrived in England from Spain. Did my history teacher at school know about these people? I don't think so – and you've got to ask why. Mary Seacole was just as much of a heroine as Florence Nightingale and made a huge contribution to nursing, yet she's overlooked. And what about the professional footballer Walter Tull, who was the first Black soldier in the British Army to lead white soldiers into battle, or Sarah Forbes Bonetta, a West African princess who was captured as a child, held in captivity and later taken to England by a British naval captain? The captain gifted Sarah to Queen Victoria, who loved her so much that she decided to become her godmother. When Sarah got married and had a child, Queen Victoria made the child her goddaughter as well.

I wish I'd learnt at school that British people of colour

had such a rich history – and while we're about it, there's also a lot of British Indian, Jewish and Chinese history that we don't know about either. It's a mystery, really, especially as it makes our history even more enthralling than it already is.

If important people of colour were incorporated into the school curriculum, there's a good chance that young Black people and people of colour might feel seen. It could give them a sense of belonging and being part of things – maybe encourage them to think, I can aspire and do amazing things as well.

How good would that be?

Out of my conversation with Sue Walton came my first ever documentary, *Alison Hammond: Back to School*. I travelled the UK investigating forgotten Black figures in UK history. Making it was an absolutely brilliant experience and it aired in November 2020. I was very proud to have presented it.

This Morning

People ask me, 'How do you think you've done so well?'

You know, I think I had a really good grounding, from the Central Junior Television Workshop to Theatre In Education and working as an entertainments rep for Airtours. Even just learning about customer service in regular jobs nudged me closer to becoming a presenter. I never settled in a job until I started with *This Morning*, and when I look back, it feels as if I'd been training for it all my life. Everything was leading me towards *This Morning*.

I was twenty-seven when I started on the show and it was the perfect time: I was ready. Fast-forward nineteen years and I was thrilled when I learnt that I'd landed the Friday presenting job. Of course, it was a bittersweet moment because my mum wasn't here to share my good news with me and Mum would have been the first person I told. I know she'd have been over the moon about it, because she loved everything about *This Morning* – right from back in the day. Oh, my goodness, she would have been so, so proud of me.

At the same time, I felt – and still feel – her guiding me and helping me with all the good and bad things that come along. So if I make any mistakes on air, don't blame me, blame Maria, lol!

I was very flattered to be asked to do this job and it almost feels as if I've come full circle since Dermot interviewed me for *Big Brother's Little Brother* when I came out of the *Big Brother* house. Remember that? He told me I should go into children's TV presenting. How wrong he was! He didn't have a clue.

We liked each other back then, but we didn't stay in touch and I didn't really know him when we started presenting *This Morning* together. We couldn't go out during lockdown. We couldn't pop out for a quick dinner or spend time in each other's homes, getting to know each other. I had to get to know Dermot live in front of the nation. It was a brand new relationship. In fact, in the beginning it felt like an arranged marriage! I was fine with that, actually: I'd finally found the husband I'd been looking for. Okay, he was a TV husband – a *married* TV husband – but he was *my* married TV husband, so I was happy. But as time has passed, we've become more like brother and sister, which is the way most marriages go, let's be honest.

The ratings have been great and people see us as a successful duo. There have even been comparisons to Ant and Dec, but only because our initials are also A and D. Admittedly one of us is taller and the other is shorter, but I can't see any other similarities. We're a lot more like Laurel and Hardy than Ant and Dec.

How does it work being a presenter? Well, on live morning programmes like *This Morning*, your brief is sent to you the night before, at about nine o'clock. Obviously, you want to go to bed then, don't you? So you try to read your brief quickly. But there are quite a lot of pages! It's like you're prepping for a major exam at the last minute: you're learning about everything that's going to be on the show and all the background on your guests. You read it through at nine o'clock at night. Then in the morning you read through it again and the next thing you know you're doing your makeup, you're doing your hair and . . .

That's the prep – and then we take the exam from 10 a.m. until 12.30 p.m., in front of all the viewers, live – and what's crazy about it is that there's no rehearsal. You're just straight up and you have to make it look easy. The only way to do that is to get out there, fly by the seat of your pants and just have fun.

On our first day, I was nervous about doing the show with Dermot, because we'd only ever done one or two shows together before, in the summer of 2020. My nervousness showed, and if you watch it back, you'll see that right at the very end, when I was winding up and telling people what would be on next week's programme, I had to say something along the lines of 'There's someone coming in on Monday . . .'

There's a 'hard count' at the end of the show, where they count down from ten and you absolutely have to finish by the time they get to zero. On that first day, I was so stressed by the whole crescendo that I didn't give myself enough time, so I ended up saying, 'On Monday's show there's going to be a woman. Have a good weekend. See you, bye!'

And that was it.

It's been very strange doing this show with Covid, because me and Dermot can't touch – we have to stay two metres away from each other. Guests are down the line, instead of in the studio. So many factors have made it difficult for us to find our feet and grow and blend, but I'm really enjoying doing the show with him now. I'm loving it. Chemistry doesn't just happen: it grows. And the chemistry is coming. I feel like we're entwining. We really are getting into our stride. We're not talking over each other now. I know when he's going to want to take things away. I know what makes him tick.

We've had this arranged marriage and now it's coming into its own: long may it blossom!

Dermot is a compassionate and kind person. He's a lovely man and I trust him; there's the respect too. He picks me up when I need a little bit of help and I pick him up when he needs a little bit of help. He's my safety net when I go off into the danger zone. We're nothing like Eamonn and Ruth, but that's okay. It feels like a great partnership.

I look forward to going into the makeup room at the studios on a Friday morning. I get in first, 7.30 a.m. to 7.45, because I like to get my makeup and hair done. Dermot comes in at about eight o'clock, puts some music on and we all start dancing. We don't even say hello. After our dance, we sit down and have a little gossip. It's really nice bonding time. I'll ask about his son and see photos of his family and he'll do the same. That's been our social life, really!

At the end of the show, as everyone knows, there's always a cook: maybe James Martin, Phil Vickery or Clodagh McKenna. Dermot and I have our food, finish the show and literally stay where we are, eating. We don't go anywhere. All the lights go down, the crew comes in and starts having a meeting – they just ignore us and we're in our little bubble, at the breakfast bar at *This Morning*, eating and chatting in our little restaurant. That's our other bit of bonding time.

There's a nervous energy with every single show I ever do because it's live, it's important and it means a lot to me. If I didn't have those nerves, it would worry me, because it would mean I didn't care – and I care a lot about *This Morning*. The show is the viewers. It's their show, not ours. It's not Dermot and Alison's show: it belongs to the *This Morning* audience. They watch it and we're just there guiding them through it so that they can enjoy it, and it's a pleasure interacting with them.

Once Dermot and I found our stride, it was just lovely to be myself and have fun, spread my wings and fly. The more fun I have, the more the viewers have fun. What else can you ask for than to do a job where you're just having fun? It's a lovely, liberating feeling – it's amazing. As the papers love to say, we're on a lol.

Happiness

I'm often asked the secret to staying positive. Everybody's different, but I enjoy life's little pleasures – things like going for a walk and smelling the fresh dew in the morning. There are some lovely trees at the back of my house and I often sit and listen to the birds and watch the squirrels have little fights. I've also got a woodpecker that pecks at the tree trunks. It's such a lovely sound.

It probably makes me seem a bit like a Miss World contestant, but I love seeing others happy and doing well in their lives. I'm always wanting to help my friends, meet new people and face new challenges. Most of all, I enjoy the special moments I have with my son, Aidan, when we connect and talk about our day and where we're at. I relish the happy feeling I get when we're doing things that Aidan enjoys: when I go and watch him kart racing, which he has a passion for, and when I'm timing him with a stopwatch to see if he can beat his best time.

Recently, we've been watching the BBC1 show *I Can See Your Voice* together. And it's not because I'm on it, either! What I love is that my son comes down and watches it with me because he genuinely likes the show. Normally, he'd be on his Xbox and I'd be downstairs watching something on Netflix, but this is a show that's actually bringing us together as a family.

What's great about it is that it's simple and good – and when something is simple and good, how can you go wrong? Those good, simple ideas are the best. Things don't need to be complicated and massively intricate. Who's a good singer and who's a bad singer? That's the premise of the show, and I can't believe how much it's blown up. People have really loved it.

When I'm watching *I Can See Your Voice* with Aidan – maybe my brother will pop in and watch it with us – it makes me remember that although I've lost my mum, I've still got the rest of my lovely family.

What Mum taught me will always live inside me – and I think my son's got it too when I look at the way he lives his life. With my mum and with Aidan, everything always seems to come from love. And love is the answer to everything.

I think it's important to be comfortable in your skin. I mean, sometimes I'm not happy with the size I am, but that's not going to prevent me enjoying my life. My life is not going to stop until I reach a certain weight because I might never get there. At whatever point in life I am, I will embrace exactly who I am, as I am. I would rather die as a gladiator in the arena of life than sit on the sidelines being a spectator of my own life. So live your life, people, and don't worry who's watching.

I'm always reminding myself to enjoy my life the way it is and appreciate what I've got. I'm a one-off – there's only one of me. There's no other person like me. How amazing is that? Each one of us is unique. There's no one else like you. It's incredible.

I hope you've enjoyed reading this book and learning a little bit more about me. And I hope you've had some laughs along the way. You've got to laugh – I can't go a day without laughing. I've always said that a day is wasted without laughter.

Now, if you're having trouble finding something to smile about, all you've got to do, guys, is fake it until you make it. Put your hands on your stomach and say, 'Ho, ho, ho,' over and over, until, all of a sudden, you'll feel so stupid that you're standing there with your hands on your stomach, saying, 'Ho, ho, ho,' that you'll naturally start laughing.

Have a lovely day! And remember, you're a one-off.

Lots of love, A.

Acknowledgements

I'd like to thank God, for making this happen in the first place. In you all things are possible.

Thanks to everyone who helped me with this book. First of all, I would like to thank Rebecca, who helped me put it together – your brilliance knows no bounds. I still can't believe we haven't met – I have learnt so much from you when it comes to writing. Thank you for being the best teacher of literacy, it was an honour to work with you.

Thanks to Transworld and Penguin Random House for believing there was anything interesting to write about. It's just been lovely working with you. I'm so happy I chose you to be my publishers; my purple quill pen is the best present I've ever had.

Frankie, my editor, you're so clever! Why? Well, because you said yes to me becoming an author. Thanks, babs, I love ya!

Thank you to Becca Barr Management, such an incredible team who have been consistent through and through, always working in my best interests. Thank you for always knowing my worth and also for being wonderful friends – you have always had my back and have been a rock to me through the years. I love you all so much. Thanks for the love and encouragement and for being a support when times weren't great. Becca, Jack, Dru, Lilly (Lolly), Vicky.

Thanks to my sister Saundra for letting me bother you over and over, picking your brains about memories I couldn't quite remember. I always want to make my big sister proud, and if I could be a fraction of the woman you are, I know I'd be happy. My brother Nicky – thanks for being the best brother ever, thanks for the protection and the secondhand clothes. I definitely get my coolness from you. I love you with all my heart, Nick.

Thank you, Anthony, Ali, Alisa and Elizabeth . . . sisters and brothers from other mothers. Thanks for loving me.

Thanks to Tamsin Eames for your input into this book; recalling our memories was hilarious.

Thank you, Kevin Lygo, Emma Gormley and Martin Frizell, for being wonderful and giving me such wonderful opportunities in television. I will always be grateful for your guidance, love and help within the industry.

To Martin Harper – you always believed in me from the very beginning, you truly are a talent and your dedication doesn't go unnoticed by me.

To Tony Gerroni and Bash, the best chauffeurs. Now if you were to write a book, that would be a good read! Thanks for getting me everywhere on time and then back to my baby.

To Dermot O'Leary – what a way to meet, during Covid. Thanks for being so lovely and dry.

Sarah Cox – 'Full-Bodied: The Band' will happen one day!

Emma Gilbert – love ya, Emma.

Josie Gibson – my spirit animal, love you.

Jason Watkins – my number-one fan.

To my lovely friends and colleagues: Holly, Phillip,

Eammon, Ruth, Gok, Rylan, Rustie, Deirdre, Nick, Eva, Bryony, Alice, Zoe, Ranj, Rochelle, Steve, Phil V, Sharon, Toff, Gyles, Judi, Charlene W, Chizzy, Oti, Tameka, Jenny, Judy, Sunectra, Frankie, Pixie, Caroline, Aljaž, Angelica, Scott, Georgina, Vanessa, Lisa, Jeff, Kathryn, Matt, Nick, Chris H, Chris K, Fluer, Jane, David, Rachel, Michelle, Amber, Emily, Ateh, Nicole, Chelsea, Ollie, Johnathan, Ashleigh, Daisey, Ken, Tony, Verina, Clodagh, Sarah, Bev, Matthew, John, James, Nisha, Mohamed, Richard, Gerald, Shervon, Charlene, Leigh, Andrew, Miranda, Louise, Debs, Lorraine, Lex, Mariam, Janice, Sam, Will, Harry, Jay, Anna, Uma, Maya, Kika, Jo, Jamie.

To Clive Bennett: thanks for loving my mum the way you did. I will always hold you in special regard. Thanks for being a grandad to Aidan and a father figure to me. Love you always.

To Sheldon Community Church – especially the Akins family! Thanks for the love and for baptizing me. I will never forget you bringing me to God's word.

To Central Television Workshop – I definitely wouldn't be where I am today without the workshop. *Taxi!!*

To Colin Edwards, Ladene, Susie, Jackie, Seth, Gerald, Sharon, Darren, Graham, Mark, Tim, Chung, Semone, Matthew Hickin, Ross, Ester, Gem, Michelle. Sally, Jenny, Heather, Kelly and Harriet – you all hold a special place in my heart. The jokes we had will never be repeated. Your secrets are safe with me, but I will put them into my novel . . .

Photo-cover glam squad – the best glam team by a mile and so much fun to be around. You are literally dream-team goals, Mikey Phillips, Michelle Sultan.

Stevie B and Victoria photography and video. Dan Williams and Nicky Johnston (candle dream-maker by night).

Thanks to Warren Farm School: Marie, Celia, Geraldine, Lorraine, Dawn. To Cardinal Wiseman RC Secondary School: Mrs Coleman (RIP), Emily, Susan and Eammon. And to St Phillips RC College: Angelica, Matt and Polly.

To Nourddine: you did actually give me the best birthday present ever. I love our son Aidan so much – thank you for loving him in the only way you knew how. We are always here for you, your wife and Aidan's brother and sisters.

To Laura-Marie and Scott: thanks for taking care of Alison Hammond fans on Facebook. You are both incredible!

To Aidan: what can I say about you, young man? I have always been incredibly proud of you and have just loved watching you grow into the handsome, intelligent, funny and kind man you are today. Keep doing what you're doing and I know you will be fine. This is all for you, son! My world.

To George Floyd. I know by losing your life, my life mattered that little bit more. It feels so unfair that it took your violent death to open the eyes and hearts of others. You will never be forgotten. God bless and RIP.

I love you, Mum.

Credits

This book is a work of non-fiction based on the life, experiences and recollections of the author. In some cases, names of people, places, dates, sequences and the detail of events have been changed to protect the privacy of others.

Lyrics on p. 11 from 'Maria' from the musical *West Side Story*, music written by Leonard Bernstein and lyrics by Stephen Sondheim.

Lyrics on p. 18 from 'I'm Gonna Wash That Man Right Outa My Hair' from the musical *South Pacific*, music written by Richard Rodgers and lyrics by Oscar Hammerstein.

Lyrics on p. 107 from 'Heaven Is A Place On Earth', written by Rick Nowels and Ellen Shipley and recorded by Belinda Carlisle.

Lyrics on p. 259 from 'I'm Every Woman', written by Nickolas Ashford and Valerie Simpson, produced by Narada Michael Walden, David Cole and Robert Clivillés, and recorded by Whitney Houston.

Lyrics on p. 332 from 'And I Am Telling You I'm Not Going' from the musical *Dreamgirls*, music written by Henry Krieger and lyrics by Tom Eyen.

Lyrics on p. 332 from 'Work', written by PartyNextDoor, Rihanna, Drake, Monte Moir, Rupert 'Sevn' Thomas, Allen Ritter and Matthew Samuels, produced by Boi-1da, Kuk Harrell and Noah '40' Shebib, and recorded by Rihanna featuring Drake.

Known for her quick wit, outrageous presenting style and infectious laugh, Alison Hammond has been a much-loved fixture on British television for two decades. She joined *This Morning* in 2003 and has since secured some of the most watched – and loved – celebrity interviews ever. She's tap-danced with Renée Zellweger, rapped with Will Smith, jammed with Russell Crowe, and been serenaded by Hugh Jackman.

In 2021, she became one of *This Morning*'s main hosts, alongside Dermot O'Leary, and also appeared on a new BBC Saturday-night primetime entertainment show, *I Can See Your Voice*, alongside fellow judges Amanda Holden and Jimmy Carr, and host Paddy McGuinness.

From her rise to fame on Channel 4's *Big Brother* in 2002, to her appearances on *I'm a Celebrity . . . Get Me Out of Here!*, *Strictly Come Dancing* and *Celebrity Great British Bake Off*, Alison's warmth, honesty and joy have made her one of the most popular presenters on TV today.

A Q&A with Alison Hammond

1. **Congratulations on becoming an author! What was the experience of writing your first book like?**

I really enjoyed writing the book and remembering stories from the past. I'm normally the sort of person who lives for now and I don't really look back, so this has actually been a really lovely experience.

2. **Your book contains lots of real memories about your friends and family. How did they react when you told them you'd be writing about them?**

It's weird because I was worried that they wouldn't want their stories in the book, but when I told family and friends they were in my book they were really overwhelmed and so excited and flattered to have been considered. They said, 'I can't believe you put me in your book!' and I was like, 'You're an amazing part of my story and you made me who I am today.' I had to get permission from Josie and she just could not believe I had put her in the book. She said, 'I'm so flattered.'

3. How did you find time for writing in your busy schedule?

Voice notes on my phone were so helpful while I was writing the book. Whenever thoughts or memories came up, I would literally go to my notes on my phone and voice-note my thoughts so that I wouldn't forget. My phone has been very helpful to me. On some days I actually liked sitting at my desk and working as it made me more focused.

4. Do you have any words of wisdom for your readers?

There are three things you need in life:
1. Something to do.
2. Someone to love.
3. Something to dream of for the future.
Have all three and you're rocking!

5. You always say 'a day is wasted without laughter'. Can you tell us about something that has made you smile recently?

That I'll be seeing Dermot soon :-)